KIDS
CAMP!

KIDS CAMP!

Activities for the Backyard or Wilderness

LAURIE CARLSON

and JUDITH DAMMEL

CHICAGO
REVIEW
PRESS

Library of Congress Cataloging-in-Publication Data
Carlson, Laurie M., 1952–
    Kids camp! : activities for the backyard or wilderness /
Laurie Carlson and Judith Dammel. — 1st ed.
        p. cm.
        Includes bibliographical references (p.   ).
        ISBN 1-55652-237-1
        1. Camping—Equipment and supplies—Juvenile literature.
2. Outdoor recreation for children—Juvenile literature.
I. Dammel, Judith.   II. Title
    GV191.76.C37 1995
    796.54—dc20   94-41030
                                                                        CIP
                                                                        AC

The author and the publisher disclaim all liability incurred in
connection with the use of the information contained in this book.

Interior illustrations by Sean O'Neill
Typography by MobiGraphics, Inc., Chicago, Illinois

First edition
Published by Chicago Review Press, Incorporated
814 North Franklin Street
Chicago, Illinois 60610
ISBN 1-55652-237-1
Printed in the United States of America

5 4 3 2

For Rachel and Tom

Contents

A NOTE TO GROWN-UP CAMPERS

Remember your childhood—climbing over rocks, searching for birds' nests, and puzzling over animal tracks in the mud? Remember the daydreams of finding gold as you dug in the dirt and searching for wolf packs or giant bears as you hiked through brushy woods?

Many of us have those memories because we had the time and opportunity to wander in the natural world. Today's children have little, if any, contact with nature, let alone the "wild." Jaded, badgered by advertisers, locked safely in their homes, children are being short-changed. And, understandably, children aren't always free to explore nature—it's seldom around the corner.

Many children have become the recipients of a synthesized natural experience. They observe nature via books and videos without dipping a toe in an icy brook or smelling wildflowers. They wear rain forest T-shirts, but have never enjoyed plucking shiny pebbles from a stream, crawling after a bulbous toad, or picking and eating wild berries.

Children need nature; they need to touch it, hear it, and taste it. They need the simple experiences: playing in piles of freshly cut grass, feet in soft mud, a caterpillar wiggling down a finger. These things are now often the most difficult for us to provide. It isn't easy trying to find twigs or pebbles, let alone trees to climb or places to fish, when we live in tightly secured, manicured, and planned housing structures. Nature can't be purchased in stores or by mail order, or sent on a fax machine. We have to go out of our way to provide some time to wander, picnic, camp, or hike. These true experiences can't be synthesized.

Contact with nature gives children a chance to realize they can make a difference. They can see their immediate control and effect on the world around them when they fill birdfeeders, water plants, or lift a rock just to see what's under it.

If the next generation loses touch with nature, we are all in danger. We need nature for our spirit, for our soul. Without exploring the natural world, we will not learn to cherish or even respect it. We will lose our connection to other living things, and will not care if they are destroyed.

So, take that hike, enjoy that picnic, and set out on that camping trip! You will give yourself and your child memories to treasure for a lifetime.

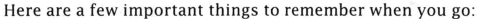

Here are a few important things to remember when you go:

Stay Safe Safety while camping is a primary concern. Nature is always changing and unpredictable, so get all the information you can about the area before you go. Ask the campground supervisor, the state park ranger, or forest service ranger if there is anything that might pose a danger. Ask what hazards might be in the area: weather, terrain, fire, or flood. Are there animal problems with bears, cougars, or poisonous snakes? Ask the ranger about precautions for deer ticks. Follow his or her advice, use common sense and good judgment, and you'll all enjoy yourselves more.

First Aid Get a first-aid handbook (the Red Cross publishes an excellent one) and a first-aid kit with extra supplies for whatever may come up. Use common sense, and be prepared.

Know the Rules Find out ahead of time whether animals or plants are protected and can't be gathered. Know if you are on public or private property and what the rules are. Learn what's allowed in your campground—pets, campfires, or when lights should be turned out, for example.

Supervise Children at All Times There is always the possibility a child will become lost, and the results can be very serious. Be firm about the rules against leaving camp alone. Try to "lose-proof" your older child ahead of time with instructions about what to do. Never allow young children to wander away from camp alone; it's an exciting time for them, but you are ultimately responsible for their safety. Realize that in mountainous areas dark falls rapidly after sundown—take no chances!

Find Out Get some field guides for plants, animals, and rocks so that you can help your child identify things he or she sees. Maps and guides are available from forest rangers, campground supervisors, and local bookstores.

Respect the Outdoors Think green—remember your impact on nature, and teach your child how to leave things in better shape than you found them.

Respect Other Campers A campground is a small community, so be a good citizen. Pets, noise, litter, and rude behavior can disrupt everyone else's enjoyment.

Make the Most of It Try to enjoy everything; even a rainstorm can become an event when remembered back home next winter! Family camping can be a wonderful way to introduce your kids to the wonders of nature and to enjoy each other's company.

A NOTE TO
KID CAMPERS

Camping out, whether you go for the day or overnight, is a lot of fun. Hiking through the woods, searching for insects under a log, and finding pebbles by a stream are all a part of camping. It's amazing how much you will learn about nature while you're enjoying yourself. Remember that you are a part of nature, too, and it's important for you to learn about it.

This book is full of activities to do so that you can have fun camping and discover new things at the same time. To get the most from this book, read it before you go and pick out the activities you want to try at camp. Then, gather the supplies and tools you'll need to take along to do the projects.

Here are some simple things to remember:

Be Careful What You Eat Don't eat any plant or berry unless an adult who knows what it is tells you it's OK. If they're not sure, don't pick it.

Pitch In Help out with all the chores. It will be easier for everyone, and more fun.

Respect Nature Leave it cleaner than you found it, and never destroy plants, animals, or their homes.

Stay With a Grown-Up Don't walk away from camp without an adult. It's very easy to get lost, and difficult to find your way back in the outdoors.

> ***Nature Note*** *The outdoors is our precious resource, and by camping out you can learn about it firsthand.*

GET READY, GET SET...PACK UP!

Clothes to Take

Take clothing that will keep you warm when it's cold, or cool when the day heats up. Weather that is sunny in the daytime can turn cold at night. Sunny weather can turn to rain or hail when a cloud blows in. It's important to take clothing that is practical rather than cute.

When you are deciding on clothing to take, think of clothes that you can "layer." Take a loose-fitting coat that can be worn over a T-shirt, sweatshirt, and sweater. When you dress this way, you can add a heavier shirt over the shirt you are wearing when it turns cooler instead of changing into a completely new shirt. You will be warmer when the weather turns really nippy.

Sit down and make a list of what clothing you will need. Start from the head and work down to the feet.

For your head you will need a hat with a brim to keep off the sun and to protect you from the heat. You will need a rainhat if your raincoat or poncho does not have one. You will need a winter hat, such as a knitted stocking hat, to wear at night or when it is cool. Wear it to bed to keep you toasty warm. It is important to keep your head covered when it's cold because you lose a great deal of body heat through your head.

It is a good idea to take a light shirt, such as a T-shirt, for those warm sunny days. If it is hot where you are camping, you should still wear a shirt to protect you from getting sunburned. To keep cool, you can dip the T-shirt in water and wear it wet.

You will need a long-sleeved shirt to put on over your T-shirt when you start to feel cool. A sweatshirt or flannel shirt is great. Over this you may want to layer a warm sweater or heavier sweatshirt. When the air turns really cool, you will want to wear your loose-fitting coat over these. This is probably enough to take for normal weather. In case of rain, you will want to take a rainhat, poncho, or raincoat.

Legs also need to be protected from the weather. A pair of shorts with pockets are handy for your journal, magnifying glass, pencil, and map. You can wear warm-ups over them, too. When the weather turns cold, a pair of long underwear underneath the sweatpants can warm up your legs. If the air is very cold, wear your long underwear, warm-ups, and another pair of pants over them.

You won't need to wear this much clothing often, but it's a good idea to be prepared. Be sure that your clothing is loose and comfortable. If the layers are squeezed too tightly the air will not circulate and you will not stay as warm. Jeans are not a good choice as they can become wet with the dew and rain. When denim material is wet your pants are heavy, cold, and tight on your legs. Denim also takes a long time to dry out. A loose pair of pants made out of wool or wool-blend would be perfect.

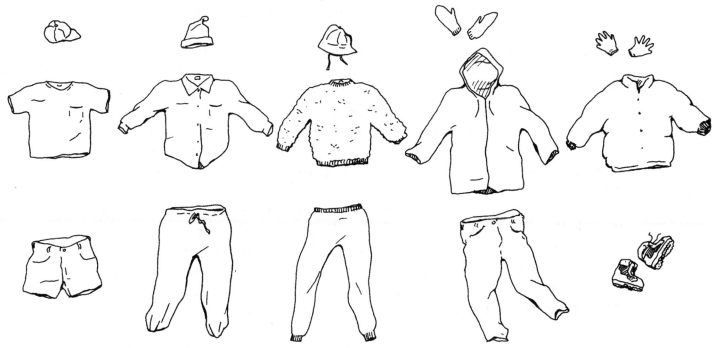

Good Idea   *Take along a bandana. Use it as a sunshade, washcloth, packsack, or towel—two or three can even make a swimsuit!*

Hands and feet also need protection. Hands get cold, and a pair of mittens or gloves will do the job. Gloves are nice when you need to use all your fingers. If you don't need to use individual fingers, mittens will keep your hands warmer.

Feet are one of the most important parts of the body when you're hiking. Blisters caused by wet feet or poorly fitting shoes can keep you from enjoying the hike. Take enough pairs of socks to always have dry socks on your feet. It is a good idea to wear two pairs of stockings. A thin stocking to wear under heavy wool socks is ideal. Make sure there are no wrinkles or holes so that the socks fit comfortably.

Now, most important—shoes. Soft hiking boots are much better than hard leather ones. Hard leather boots take a long time—sometimes years—to break in, and, until they are comfortable, you will suffer from blisters. Soft hiking boots can often be worn right out of the store with no problem. When you go to buy new boots, bring the socks that you plan to wear, and try on the boots over those socks. The boots should not rub or pinch your feet. Walk around the store. Do your heels move up and down as you walk? If they do, then the boots are too big. Do your toes pinch as you walk? This means that the boots are too small or too tight across the toes. Have a knowledgeable salesperson help you with the fit.

If you don't have hiking boots, tennis shoes will usually do fine, unless you plan on hiking many miles over steep or rocky terrain. Make sure that your shoes fit well and that they don't have holes. If you can't fit two pairs of socks under them, pick out one pair of comfortable socks. The socks should not have any holes that could rub your skin. Take two pairs of shoes along. If one pair gets wet, it can dry while you wear the other pair.

Clothes to Make

The section before this one, "Clothes to Take," talks about choosing the proper clothing to take on your camping adventure. It's always important to be prepared for any type of weather or terrain. You would not want being cold or wet to get in the way of the world of fun that's waiting for you in nature.

You probably will have to buy or borrow most of the clothes that you take out into the great outdoors; however, here are a couple of suggestions for clothes you can create. These things are easy and fun to make, and you can tell your family and friends that you did it yourself.

Poncho

MATERIALS

Plastic tarp or
vinyl shower curtain

Velcro strips

Markers

Scissors

Heavy-duty glue,
or needle and thread

Make a simple poncho to protect you from rain showers. Spread a plastic tarp or vinyl shower curtain out on the floor, and fold it in half. Lie on it with your arms spread out along the fold. Have a friend mark where your wrists are on the plastic.

Cut the poncho to make a square long enough to cover your arms. Cut a hole in the center just large enough to fit your neck through, and cut the front open. Use glue, or needle and thread, to attach Velcro pieces along the front opening.

Warm Woolies

MATERIALS

Pair adult-sized wool socks
Marker
Scissors
Needle and thread

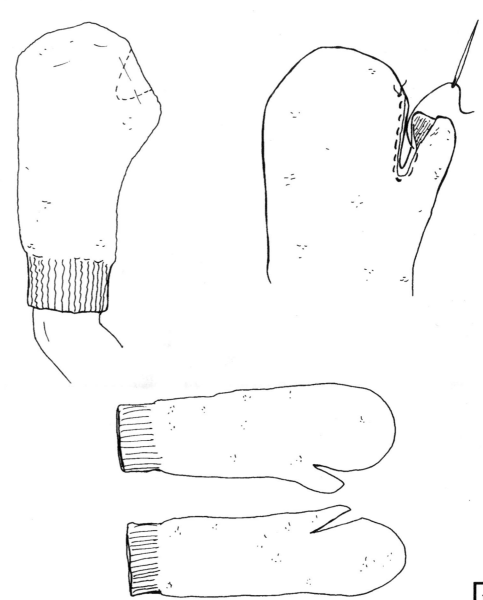

Turn a sock inside out and put it over your hand. Draw a "V" between your thumb and your index finger, leaving some space around your thumb for sewing. Cut along the line through both sides of the sock. Use your needle and thread to sew the cut edges together. Make small stitches to prevent it from unraveling. Repeat with the other sock. Turn right side out and wear!

> **Good Idea** *Stuff your clean clothes in a pillowcase, fasten with a rubber band, and you have an instant pillow.*

Make Your Own Camp Gear

Camping out means you get to live a bit differently than you do at home, but you still need a comfortable place to sleep, dishes and storage containers for food, packs to carry stuff in, and first-aid supplies.

Plan ahead for your trip. Think about where you are going to camp. What will the weather be like? What activities do you plan to do? What things will you need? Make a list and sort out the items you plan to take. What will you borrow, buy, or make?

Before you pack, set aside some time to make some of your own gear. It's fun to put it together yourself. Here are some ideas for things you can make before you go, and they really work.

Make It with Jugs

You can make useful camping equipment easily with old plastic milk jugs. Try a bowl, plate, or funnel—or make up your own jug gear.

MATERIALS

Plastic milk jugs
Scissors or craft knife

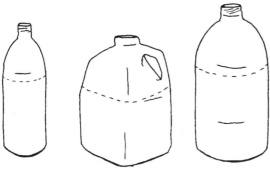

Try bottles of any size.

Make a cup.

Cut away the bottom of a plastic jug to make a lightweight, unbreakable camp bowl. Trim it shorter to make a plate, or a Frisbee-like toy to toss.

Trim the top part from a plastic bottle and make a funnel for fun at the beach. Use the bottom for a drinking glass.

Make a funnel.

Use it to fill containers.

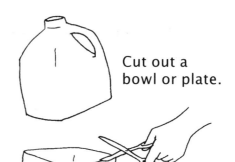

Cut out a bowl or plate.

Backyard Bedroll

MATERIALS

2 thick blankets
15 large safety pins
Ruler

Pin 2 blankets together like this.

Lay one blanket flat on the floor. Lay the second blanket on top placing it slightly higher than the first so that 3 inches of the first blanket show at the bottom. Fold the top blanket in thirds. Pin down the free edge of the blanket with 4 safety pins.

Bring the bottom of the first blanket over the second blanket roll and pin with 3 safety pins.

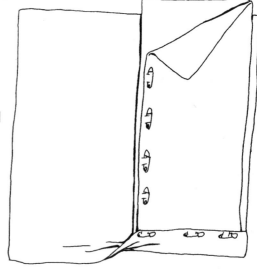

Then, fold up the bottom and pin it in place.

Fold the free half of the bottom blanket over the bedroll and pin securely with 4 pins. Fold the bottom of the bedroll under and pin securely with 4 pins. You've made your own cozy place to sleep.

Good Idea *Plan to stay warm. Sleeping bags have labels telling the temperature they are made for. Make sure you have a warm enough bag for your campsite.*

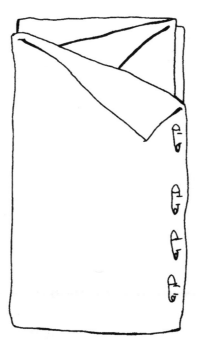

Fold the last part of the bottom blanket over and pin.

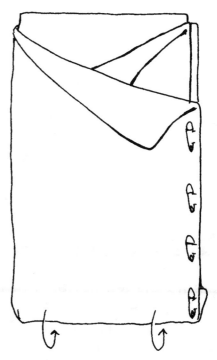

Fold down the bottom and pin.

Plenty of Ways to Pack

MATERIALS

Jeans
16 large safety pins, or heavy-
duty needle and thread
Belt
Chalk

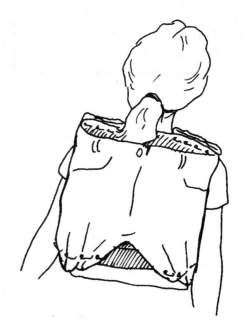

Pants Pack

 Bring the leg bottoms of the jeans up to your shoulders and securely pin them to the back waistband of the jeans, using 4 pins on each leg. Pin the bottoms only to the back of the waistband and leave the front of the waistband free. The legs will form the straps of the pack. The waistband will be the opening of your pack.

Try on your pack wearing the belt under the pack and around your waist and the leg-straps. Have a friend draw a chalk line across the legs directly below your belt. Take the pack off and pin 4 safety pins across each leg-strap on the chalk lines. These pins will prevent your gear from falling into the leg-straps.

You can stitch the pack with a needle and doubled thread instead of using the safety pins.

18

MATERIALS

Bath towel
Two 1-foot cotton cords
Sewing machine

 Fold the towel in thirds. Fold back the top flap and stitch the sides to make a pocket. As you stitch, poke the ends of the cord inside the seam at the top and bottom of the pocket. Do the same thing on the other side of the pocket. Slip your arms through the cords, and you're ready to go.

Towel Pack

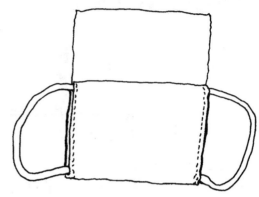

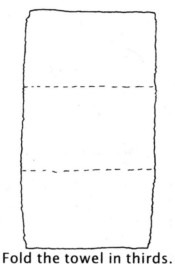

Fold the towel in thirds.

Stitch the sides catching the cords in the seam. Sew it again to reinforce the stitching.

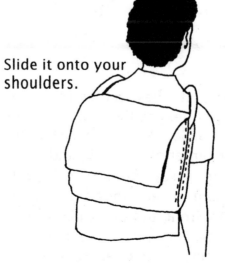

Slide it onto your shoulders.

Sack Pack

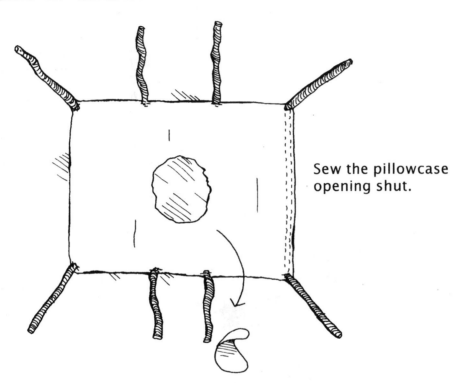

Sew the pillowcase opening shut.

MATERIALS

Pillowcase

8-foot heavy cord or lightweight rope

Needle and thread

Scissors

4 safety pins

Measuring tape

Chalk

Sew a sturdy seam, using small stitches, across the pillowcase's opening. Sew another seam right next to the first one to reinforce it. Cut the rope into eight 1-foot pieces. Sew 1 piece to each of the 4 corners of the sack. Measure the exact center of the sack, and mark it with chalk. Cut an opening in the center large enough to fit your head through. You will also use this opening to pack your gear into the pack. Put the pack on, and adjust it evenly front and back. Measure 4 inches down from each armpit front and back. Pin a safety pin at all four points. Sew a rope to the pack at each safety-pin marker. Remove the pins.

⬡ Use the can opener to punch a small hole in one side of the can, near the top edge. Turn the can halfway around and make another hole directly across from the first.

Cut off the twisted top part of the hanger. Use your pliers to grab below the part of the hanger you want to take off, and twist until it comes off. Discard this part. Straighten the rest of the hanger. Thread one end of the hanger through one of the holes and twist the end so that it holds securely. Take the other end of the hanger and put it through the other hole and twist.

If you make tin can totes out of different sizes of cans, you can stack them inside each other while traveling to and from camp. These cans will make it easy to carry water, berries, snacks, or materials you collect while hiking.

MATERIALS

Tin cans
Wire coat hangers
Punch-type can opener
Pliers (with grown-up help)

Tin Can Totes

MATERIALS

11 newspaper sheets

Three 30-gallon plastic
garbage bags

Wide transparent shipping tape

Two 2-foot ropes

Scissors

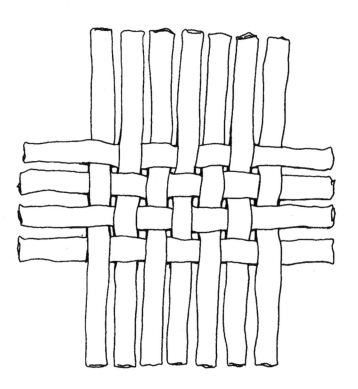

Terrific Tote Bag

Fold a newspaper sheet in half with the long ends together. Fold it in half four times to make a long strip 1½ inches wide. Tape the strip at each end and in the middle so that it won't come unfolded. Fold and tape 10 more strips.

Lay 7 strips side by side. Weave 4 strips into the middle of these 7 strips. Weave the first strip under, over, under—repeat the pattern. Weave the second strip going over, under, over—repeating. Weave the strips to form the bottom of the basket.

Cut each bag into a continuous strip measuring about 3 inches wide. Weave the garbage bag strips around the newspaper strips. As you weave, hold the newspaper strips upright to form the sides. Each time you have made a complete circle, weave 2 strips together. Do this double weave at a different place each time. Every time you have completed 3 rounds, gently push down with your fingers as you pull the newspaper strip up. This will keep the sides straight and the weave tight.

When you are near the end of a garbage bag strip, add a new one. Weave the old and new together around 6 strips. Drop the old one and continue weaving with the new one. When you reach the end of the newspaper strips, it is time to finish the basket.

Trim all the strips evenly around the basket. Cut a 7-inch strip of tape. Place the middle of the strip against the top of the basket having 3½ inches extending down the sides on the inside and outside of the basket. Press firmly. This will keep the basket from unraveling. Repeat all the way around the top until it is all taped.

Poke a hole into the basket about 1½ inches down from the edge, through the tape and the weaving. Poke the same kind of hole 2 inches along the edge. Insert one of the ropes into these holes and tie into a sturdy knot. This will form one of the handles. Repeat on the opposite side of the basket for the other handle.

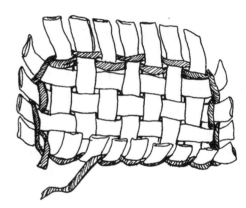

Camp Cooler

 Fill the empty mesh bag with food that you want to keep cool. This cooler is good for unopened cartons of milk, juice, pop, sealed puddings, or any food in an unopened sealed container. Don't use food that can be ruined in water.

Tie the rope around the opening of the bag with a tight knot to close the bag. Lay the filled bag in a lake, stream, or river where the water will cover it completely. Tie the other end of the rope to a strong, sturdy branch or rock on the shore. When you need food from the cooler, pull the rope and cooler onto the shore, untie the knot, and remove the food you need. Then retie the knot and put the rest back into the water.

Stay Safe *This cooler is best used for picnics and day trips. If you are camping in bear country, don't use it because the bears can smell the food through the containers and will come for it.*

MATERIALS

Plastic mesh produce bag
(the kind onions, apples, and grapefruit are sold in)
Rope

Comfy Camp Cushion

MATERIALS

Vinyl: Two 16-by-16-inch pieces (you can use a shower curtain)

Newspapers
Hole punch
Yarn and yarn needle
Scissors

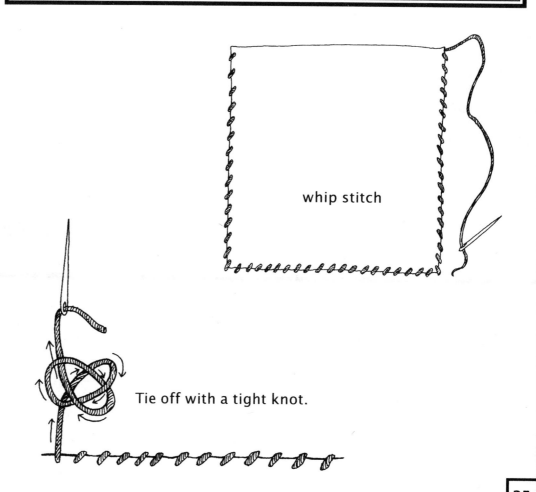

whip stitch

Tie off with a tight knot.

 Place the 2 pieces of vinyl together with the wrong sides facing each other. Punch holes through both pieces at the same time. Make the holes about one inch apart along the edges of the vinyl. Use the yarn and needle to sew 3 sides together with a whip stitch (see the illustration). Tear newspaper into strips and stuff into cushion case. Use as much newspaper as you need to achieve the amount of cushioning you want. Continue stitching around the last side with the yarn. Tie off with a tight knot and enjoy your comfy camp cushion.

Outdoor Journal

A journal is useful when you want to write about your hike, draw pictures of the insects or flowers you see, or just write poems or stories that come to you while you are surrounded by nature. This little book will fit in your pocket or backpack, and you will never lose your pencil!

Fold several sheets of paper in half.

Cut along the crease.

Stack the pages and fold them in the center. Stitch them together along the center.

Punch a hole in the book and tie on a pencil with some yarn.

MATERIALS

3 or 4 sheets of typing paper

Decorative paper for a cover: colored paper, shopping bag, gift wrap, or wallpaper

Heavy-duty needle and thread (or stapler)

12 inches of yarn

Pencil

Scissors

Hole punch

Fold the sheets of typing paper in half. Unfold them and cut along the crease. Take one of these pieces and put it on top of the decorative paper you have selected for your cover. Trace around it and cut out the cover paper so that it's the same size as the inside pages. Stack the papers together on top of the cover. Fold it in half and crease. Staple or stitch the pages and cover together along the center fold.

Punch a hole in the book and tie on a short pencil with the piece of yarn.

Soap-to-Go

MATERIALS

Bar of soap
Cord
Large nail

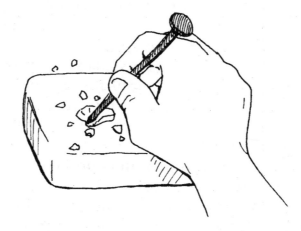

Before you go on your trip, work a hole in a bar of soap with a large nail. Tie a long loop of cord through the hole. When you get to your campsite, you can hang it from a tree branch between uses at the washing tub. Shaving cream is a great substitute for bar soap or shampoo when you're camping—it's more fun, too!

Always wash from buckets or plastic jugs of water, and never let your soap get into the stream or lake—it might harm fish and plants.

Work a hole in the soap with a nail.

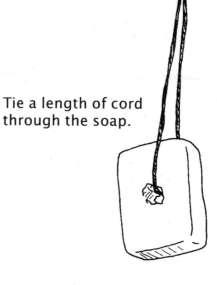

Tie a length of cord through the soap.

Pocket First-Aid Kit

MATERIALS

Bandages in different shapes
and sizes
Moleskin (from a drugstore)
Lip balm with sunscreen
Sunscreen
Foil-wrapped antiseptic wipes
First-aid antibiotic cream
Tweezers
Baking soda
Petroleum jelly (like Vaseline)
Empty 35mm film canisters
Small container to put it all in
Whistle

You can pack a little kit of necessary items for a hike or picnic. Be sure that grown-ups also have a first-aid kit!

 Assemble your supplies and put them in a small container, such as a sealable plastic bag or a lunch box. Put petroleum jelly in an empty film container: use it for insect bites, sunburn, chapped lips, and minor scrapes. Put a little baking soda in another container and use it for an insect bite, upset stomach, and for brushing your teeth. Put the antibiotic cream on any area where your skin is broken, such as blisters, cuts, scrapes, slivers, or insect bites.

You may be wondering what "moleskin" is for. You can use it to cover blisters. Blisters can be very painful and become infected, and you will want to take care of them right away so that your trip is not ruined. To treat a blister, wash and dry the skin, and put on some antibiotic cream. Cut out some moleskin in the shape of a donut. Peel the sticky paper off the moleskin and press it over the blister, making sure that the hole is directly over the blister. Cover the moleskin patch with a bandage. To get ready for your camping trip, cut up several of these little moleskin donuts, but leave the paper on the sticky side until you need them.

Wear a hat to shade your face and sunscreen at all times, even when the day is cloudy. At high altitudes, like in the mountains, sunburns occur more rapidly than at low altitudes because the sun is stronger. Sun is also reflected by snow and light-colored rocks; so, if you are surrounded by these things, you should be aware that you will burn more quickly than in a forest or grassy area. You should wear a hat with a visor or brim and sunglasses to protect yourself.

The whistle can be carried in the first-aid kit or worn on a cord around your neck or in your pocket. Use the whistle only when you need help. Blow three short, sharp bursts with the whistle and then wait a few minutes before you repeat with three more short, sharp bursts. Continue in this way until someone comes to help you. The whistle will carry farther than your voice. *Remember, this whistle is not a toy and should only be used when you are in danger or lost.*

Your pocket first-aid kit won't include all supplies you might need if you are injured, but it is great for those scratches and scrapes that can happen while you are hiking, playing, or exploring around the camp.

The grown-ups in your camping group should have a larger first-aid kit. Whenever you use items from it, be sure to replace them before your next camping trip.

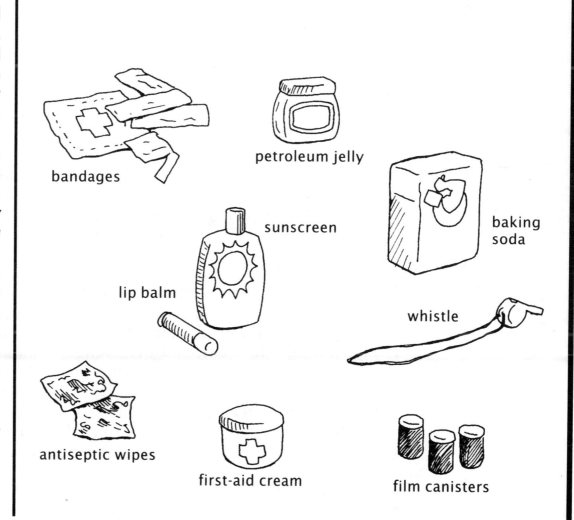

bandages

petroleum jelly

sunscreen

baking soda

lip balm

whistle

antiseptic wipes

first-aid cream

film canisters

Discovery Gear

Discovering new and unusual things makes camping all the more exciting. You're outdoors surrounded by nature, and nature is always full of surprises. Stay alert to the sounds, smells, and sights all around you. Listen to the birdcalls, the wind whistling through the trees, and the sounds at water's edge. Smell the fresh air, the flowers, even the frying bacon! Watch carefully for unusual plants and animals.

When you walk, watch underfoot for little discoveries that others may pass by: a shiny beetle, a tiny pinecone, delicate moss or lichens. Take the time to look at everything closely and you may discover that you are a born explorer!

Here are some projects for making special gear that will help you investigate nature. Make these tools before you go so that you're ready when you discover something interesting at camp.

Sifting Screen

MATERIALS

Wooden stretcher frame
for art canvas
(from an art supply store)
or old wooden picture frame

¼-inch mesh hardware cloth
or window screen, large
enough to fit over the
stretcher frame

Tacks and tack hammer
(or staple gun with grown-up help)

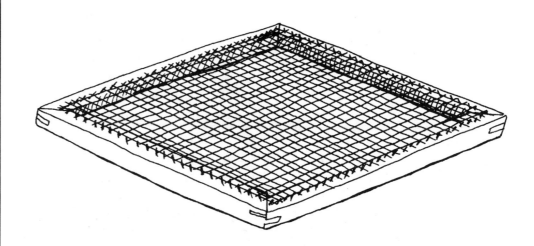

Stretch the screen across the picture frame and use the tacks and hammer to fasten it tightly. Put tacks every inch or so around the entire frame.

When you sift dirt with the screen, make sure the frame is on the bottom, with the tacked side up. Then the screen won't be torn loose by the weight of the dirt. Gently rub your hand in a back and forth motion over the dirt. This will loosen the dirt, and the particles will sift through the screen leaving the rocks, roots, and sticks. Look through your sifting—you may find rocks to add to your collection, or even fossils!

Magnifying Glass Holder

MATERIALS

2-quart milk carton
Magnifying glass
Ruler
Marker
Scissors

Nature Note *Slow down and notice everything: every blade of grass, puddle, bit of bark, and footprint. Nature is in the little things we often step over.*

Wash and dry the empty milk carton. Find the focusing distance of your glass by moving it up and down over a picture. You have found the focusing distance when you see the picture clearest through the glass. While keeping the glass in this position, measure the distance from the glass to the picture with a ruler. Measure the same distance from the bottom of the milk carton, and mark it. Using a ruler, draw a straight line around all four sides of the carton at this mark. Cut along this line.

Cut a square hole a little smaller than your magnifying glass in the bottom of the milk carton. Make 1-inch cuts in the edge of the carton 2 inches in from each corner. Cut a straight line from each cut to the other cut on the same side. These cuts will form the 4 legs of the holder.

Turn the carton over so that the bottom is the top. Lay your glass on top of the hole and take a look at something tiny: a petal, grain of sand, or mosquito. Amazing!

magnifying distance

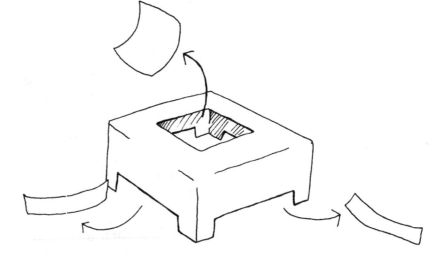

Insect Viewer

MATERIALS

Clear plastic container with lid
(like for instant coffee or
peanut butter)*

Magnifying glass
Scissors
Hammer and nail
Craft glue

*Optional: Older kids can use a
glass container.

Have an adult help you cut a hole in the lid by first making holes with a hammer and nail. Then use a craft knife to make a hole a little smaller than your magnifying glass. Poke some air holes into the lid. Glue the outside edges of the magnifying glass over the hole.

Look under rocks, beneath leaves on the ground, or on the brown curled leaves of plants to find insects. Search your campsite and you may find picnicking ants. The best way to find insects is to "become small." Sit and listen for soft rustles, turn over rocks, and wait patiently. Insects are everywhere and once you learn how to think "buggy," you will find them easily.

Remember to set all of the insects free after you have finished watching them.

Water Wonder Watcher

MATERIALS

Milk carton
Plastic wrap
Large rubber band, or
heavy-duty tape
Scissors

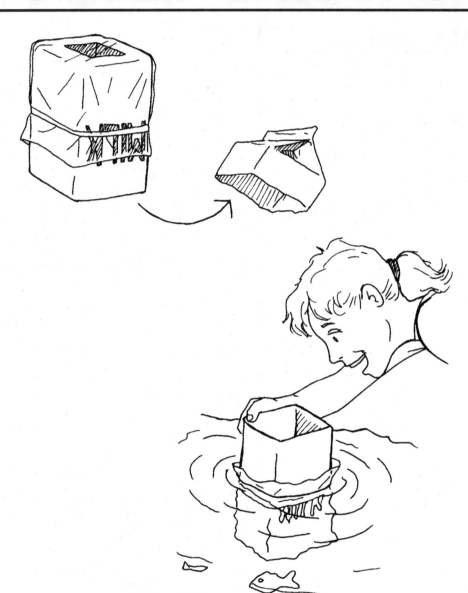

Cut away the top of the milk carton, and cut an opening in the base. Wrap plastic wrap over the opening and hold it in place with a large rubber band or tape.

To view what's beneath the dark surface of still water, lower the watcher into the water and look through the clear bottom to observe all the water wonders. Sit quietly near the water and you'll notice many little insects, tadpoles, and even baby fish!

> **Stay Safe** *Fast or deep water can be dangerous! Do not wade above your knees and stay out of fast water completely! Always let an adult know where you are.*

Fix Some Food

Whether you're headed for the wilderness or a friend's backyard, camping makes you hungry! The fresh air and exercise will perk up your appetite, so take along plenty to eat.

Remember not to bring food that will spoil or melt, or that requires complicated cooking. You won't have a microwave or refrigerator out there. Keep camp food simple, healthy, and easy to pack and fix.

The "Time to Eat" chapter later in this book has recipes for meals to make at your campsite, but here are some ideas for treats you can prepare at home ahead of time. All of them are great to keep in your pack as you hike along a trail. You never know when you're going to get a craving for a snack.

Banana Chips

MATERIALS

2 ripe bananas (no bruises!)
Knife
Cookie sheet
Nonstick cooking spray
Fork
Plastic bag or covered container

Slice the bananas into thin rounds. Spray the cookie sheet with the cooking spray. Spread the banana slices in a single layer over the cookie sheet. Cook slices in a 150-degree oven for 2 hours with the oven door open about 1 inch. Turn the slices over with the fork and bake for about 2 more hours. You will know they are done when they are hard and you can't bend them. Store these treats in a plastic bag or covered container.

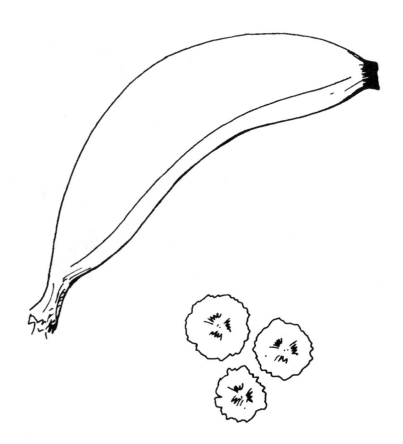

Great Gorp

MATERIALS

2 cups dry cereal
(not flakes—they crumble easily)

1 cup raisins

1 cup cut-up dried apples

1 cup dried apricots
(or banana chips, prunes,
or dates)

1 cup peanuts
(or other nuts you like)

1 cup chocolate candies
(like M&M's)

½ cup shredded coconut

Mixing bowl

Plastic sealable sandwich bags

 Mix all the ingredients in a big bowl. Pack a cupful into each plastic bag. Put a bag in your pocket or hip bag for a tasty snack while you're on the trail.

Energy Bars

MATERIALS

3 cups dried apples
2 cups dried apricots
1 cup pitted prunes
1 cup pitted dates
1 cup raisins
1 cup sunflower seeds (shelled)
¾ cup creamy peanut butter
½ cup melted margarine
½ cup honey
½ cup shredded coconut
¼ cup sesame seeds
Flour
Blender
Mixing bowl
Spoon
Plastic wrap

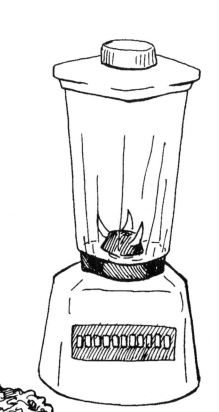

 Ask a grown-up to help chop the fruit in the blender. Chop each type of fruit separately, and put the pieces in the mixing bowl. After all the fruit has been chopped and tossed into the bowl, add the raisins, sunflower seeds, peanut butter, melted margarine, honey, coconut, and sesame seeds. Mix it all together, using your hands if you need to. Shape the mixture into small rolls with your hands and roll them in flour. Wrap each roll in a small piece of plastic wrap, and store in a covered container. Make them ahead of time and freeze until you're ready to go camping.

Fruit Leather Roll-Ups

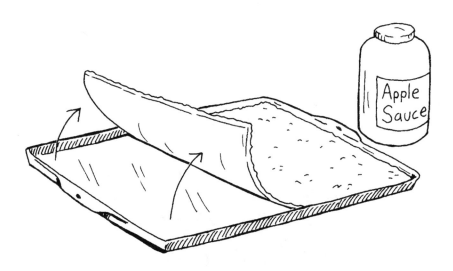

MATERIALS

30-ounce jar applesauce
1 tablespoon honey
1 teaspoon ground cinnamon
Nonstick cooking spray
Mixing bowl
Spoon
Cookie sheet
Knife
Plastic wrap

Mix the applesauce, honey, and cinnamon in a bowl with a spoon. Spray the cookie sheet with the nonstick cooking spray. Spread the mixture evenly over the whole cookie sheet. With the oven door open about 1 inch, bake at 150 degrees for 6 to 8 hours until done. When the fruit leather is done, it will be see-through, bendable, and will not be sticky when you touch it. Cut the leather into 4-by-4-inch strips. You should get about 8 strips. Lay each strip on plastic wrap and roll it all up, plastic wrap and all. Store them in a plastic bag or covered container.

Terrific Trail Mix

MATERIALS

2 cups dried cereal
(not flakes—they crumble easily)

2 cups small cheese crackers

1 cup salted peanuts

1 cup small pretzels

1 cup raisins

½ cup chocolate-covered
peanuts or raisins

¼ cup seeds
(shelled sunflower, pumpkin,
or sesame seeds)

Mixing bowl

Plastic sealable bags

Mix everything together, and then store it in individual plastic bags or one larger bag. Take along something to drink when you eat this trail mix, because the salty taste will make you very thirsty.

Hot Cocoa Mix

MATERIALS

4 cups dry powdered milk
1 cup unsweetened cocoa
1 cup sugar

Mixing bowl and spoon, or large plastic container with a lid

Plastic sealable sandwich bags

Put everything in a large bowl and mix with a spoon, or put it in a large lidded plastic container and mix it up by shaking it. Spoon 2 heaping tablespoons of mix into a sandwich bag for each person. At camp, all you need to do is stir the mix into a cup of hot water.

Super Salted Seeds

MATERIALS

2 cups pumpkin or
raw sunflower seeds in the shell

2 tablespoons cooking oil

Salt to taste

Mixing bowl

Spoon

Cookie sheet

Plastic sealable bags

Combine the seeds and cooking oil in a bowl, mixing well to coat the seeds evenly. Spread the seeds out on the cookie sheet. Shake a bit of salt on them. Bake at 250 degrees for about 45 minutes, making sure to stir the seeds every 10 minutes or so. Let them cool, and store them in plastic bags.

Tasty Tea

MATERIALS

1 ¼ cup powdered orange
drink mix (like Tang)

½ cup sugar

⅓ cup instant tea powder

½ teaspoon cinnamon

¼ teaspoon ground cloves

Plastic sealable bag,
or a container with a lid

Quart glass jar

Combine everything and store the mixture in a large plastic bag or a lidded container. To mix the tea, spoon 5 rounded teaspoons of the mix into a quart glass jar filled with water. Leave the jar of tea in the sun until it gets warm. Then, stir or shake the tea to mix it up, and pour it into a cup. Mmmm!

Apple Pocket Pies

MATERIALS

3 apples
½ cup raisins
¼ cup sugar
1 teaspoon cinnamon
2 packages refrigerator biscuits
Knife
Small mixing bowl
Spoon
Cookie sheet,
lightly greased with shortening

Flatten a biscuit.

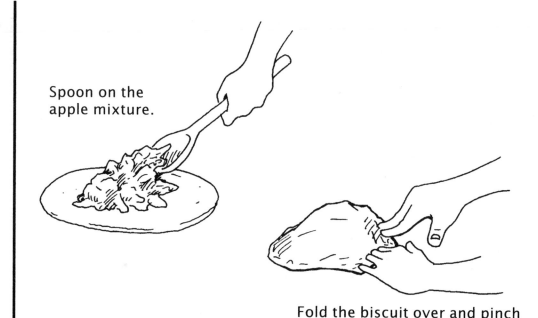

Spoon on the apple mixture.

Fold the biscuit over and pinch the edges together. Bake.

Preheat the oven to 350 degrees. Peel, core, and dice the apples with the knife. Mix the apples, raisins, cinnamon, and sugar in the bowl. Flatten the biscuits into large circles with the palm of your hand. Spoon some of the apple mixture into the center of each biscuit. Fold the biscuits over so that they form half-circles. Pinch the edges together. Place the pies on a greased cookie sheet and bake for 12 minutes, or until they turn golden brown. Remove them from the cookie sheet while they're warm. Store the baked pies in a covered container. You make them ahead of time and store them in the freezer until you go camping.

Crunchy Cheese Crackers

MATERIALS

1 pound shredded
cheddar cheese

1 ½ cups flour
(whole wheat is best)

⅓ cup sesame seeds

5 tablespoons cooking oil

5 to 6 tablespoons milk

¾ teaspoon salt

Mixing bowl

Cookie sheet, lightly rubbed
with vegetable oil

Preheat the oven to 350 degrees. Mix the cheese, flour, oil, salt, and sesame seeds in a bowl until they are well blended. Add the milk, and work the mixture into a ball with your hands. If the dough is stiff and dry, add another tablespoon of milk. Form the dough into balls the size of golf balls and flatten them between your hands. Place the crackers on the oiled cookie sheet and bake for about 20 minutes. Store in a covered container or plastic bag. These make great snacks for hiking!

Take-Along Breadsticks

MATERIALS

2 packages refrigerated biscuits
1 egg
Sesame seeds
Bowl
Fork
Pastry brush (or paper towel)
Cookie sheet, lightly greased
with shortening

 Roll each biscuit on a countertop with the palm of your hand. Stop rolling when they're about 6 inches long. Place them on a greased cookie sheet. Beat the egg in a bowl with a fork. Brush the top of each breadstick with the beaten egg—use a pastry brush or the end of a rolled-up paper towel. Sprinkle the breadsticks with sesame seeds. Bake at 350 degrees for about 6 minutes, or until they turn golden brown. Remove the breadsticks from the cookie sheet while they are still warm and let cool. Store them in a plastic bag.

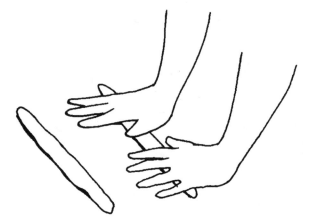

MAKE CAMP

After you've looked through this book and decided what gear, food, and activities you plan to make and do, you're ready for an outing!

Practice camping is important if you've never camped before, have new equipment, or are using equipment that you aren't sure will work. You can set everything up in the backyard and camp for the day. Day camping can be a practice session for an overnight outing or a great way to just have fun.

On a day-camping trip you can do activities, such as cooking or tent-making, that you plan to do on a longer outing. You can find out if something doesn't work, or is uncomfortable, before you find yourself far from home. An overnight camp far from home isn't the best place to discover that a needed item is back home miles away.

The first thing to do when planning your day camp is to decide where to camp. How about your own backyard, neighborhood park, or a friend's house? You can day camp by yourself, with a few friends, or with your family. Be sure your parents know what your plans are.

After you've decided where to go, you need to plan what to eat. Gather the items you will need to prepare your meal and set them in a pile ready for packing.

The next thing you must choose is clothing. For day camping, you won't need much clothing. Your regular clothing along with a jacket or raincoat if the weather is cold or rainy is fine.

The next items on your list should be equipment such as rope, a tent or tarp, a cooler, a sleeping bag or blankets, bowls, spoons, and other utensils, and anything else you will need for the day. After you've gathered all your food, clothing, and gear, pack them into your pack or tote and go camping!

> ***Good Idea*** *Use one large tent or a couple of smaller ones for the whole family. Borrow or rent one if you haven't camped before. Try it out at home first. Practice putting it up in the dark, in case you arrive at the campsite late in the day.*

When you arrive at your campsite, set up the tent so that it is ready if you want to nap or rest in the shade. Make the bed using a sleeping bag or two blankets (see page 16), set up your clothesline, and secure your food.

After you've set up the day camp, your time is free for hiking, exploring, cooking, or whatever you have planned. The most important thing about camping is to enjoy yourself! After the day is over and you are ready to return home, be sure to clean up your camp, and leave it as nice as when you arrived. (Maybe even cleaner!)

> **Good Idea**   If you've never slept in a sleeping bag or tent, try it out once at home first. If you don't have a backyard, use the living room.

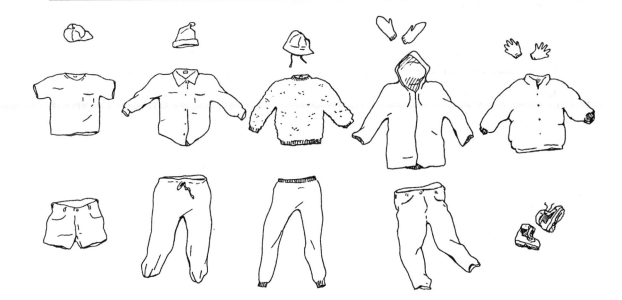

Where to Set Up Camp

The first thing to do is pick out a good place for a camp. Here are a few hints to help you pick out a camping site. Is there a good area for a tent or a tarp-tent? Are you above the water and low areas? Are the bathrooms, water, and garbage handy yet not too close? If you cannot store your food and cooking supplies in a car, are there trees where you can hang them at night and when you are away from camp? If you are planning on having a campfire, is the fire pit far enough from the sleeping area for safety?

Your campsite should have a spot large enough on high ground for your tent or tarp. Find a spot where the water will not drain into your tent if it should rain. Dry creek beds, marshy areas, areas surrounded by large boulders to channel water or any low spot are not good places to set up a tent. Choose a spot that is high enough for the water to drain away if it rains. It's no fun to wake up in the morning soaked by a suddenly-flooded tent!

If you plan on using a tarp-tent, are there trees or logs in a high area for setting one up? If not, look for another site with trees to tie the tarp to.

It is best to camp above the stream, valley, meadow, or lake. Cold air settles in the low-lying areas. You will be much warmer on a ridge or above the lake in the trees. Higher areas receive a breeze that prevents the mosquitoes from finding you so easily. If you camp right on the water, people might use your campsite as the nearest way to the water. It's best to find a place away from the beach or stream. Most campgrounds have trails to the water so that you can enjoy the water, even if you don't camp right beside it.

Stay Safe Don't drink water from lakes or streams, even if they look clean. The water contains bacteria that can make you sick.

Good Idea Make sure that the windows are open in your tent at night. If you have the tent tightly closed, your breath will condense and you will be wet by morning.

Think about shade over your camp. Mornings in camp can be cold and damp, so the morning sun is always a welcome sight. But by afternoon the sun can make the tent unbearably hot. Choose a site that is shaded in the afternoon and early evening and receives the full sun in the morning.

Before you leave home, ask the local Fish and Wildlife Agency if you might be heading for bear country. They will tell you how to safely prevent any problems.

It is handy to put your tent fairly close to the garbage, water, and bathroom. You may not want to be in the campsite right next to the bathroom because people will visit it often. A few spots away will do nicely. If the garbage cans are located next to your camp, you may be bothered by the smell or the animals who eat out of them. Locate a few sites away from the garbage. Campgrounds often have many water faucets, so it's not a problem if you camp near a faucet. Water is heavy to pack and you will use a lot of water while camping.

Set up your camp at least 100 feet away from a stream or lake. That way the animals can get their drink and you can watch them!

When you have found the ideal campsite, it's time to set up the camp. If you are setting up a tarp-tent, follow the directions for the type of tent you desire on the next few pages. When the tent is up, it's time to lay out the sleeping bags and fluff them up. Don't wait until night to lay out your sleeping bags as the longer they have to fluff up the warmer they will be. If there is room in the tent, you can also store your clothing and the totes or packs that are emptied of all food, cooking equipment, medicines, and cosmetics. If you happen to store any of these items in the tent, you could find an unwelcome guest in your bed!

After you have your sleeping area in shape, food stored, and clothing stowed away, it's time to have some fun!

Good Idea   *Get there early so that you have time to explore and get settled. It's no fun arriving at the campground late and trying to set up a tent in the dark, or finding that all the campsites have been taken.*

Tents from a Tarp

Two-Tree Tent

MATERIALS

Tarp
Rope
Tent pegs or sturdy sticks
Hammer or heavy rock

Tie a rope to two trees. Place the middle of the tarp over the rope so that both sides hang down evenly. Tie several short pieces of rope to the holes along the edge of the hanging sides of the tarp. Tie each rope onto a tent peg or a sturdy short stick. Pull the tarp tight and pound the pegs firmly into the ground.

Here are three ways to make a tent from a tarp. The first uses two trees spaced far enough apart to set up a tent, the second uses one tree, and the third needs a log or boulder.

The tent that uses the log or boulder is very low to the ground and should be used only when there are no standing trees that you can tie your tarp to. Tarp-tents aren't as waterproof as regular tents but will work very well in most weather. Be sure your tarp is waterproof, and that it's not set up on low-lying ground that might become wet in a storm. If you have an extra tarp, use it as a floor in your tarp-tent. Lay the tarp on the ground and place sleeping bags on top of the tarp to keep your sleeping bag dry.

One-Tree Tent

 Tie one end of a long rope high on a tree as far up as you can reach. Place the middle of the tarp over the rope. Tie the free end of the rope to a very strong tent peg or sturdy stick. Pull the rope away from the tree until you have the tarp in the desired position. Pound the peg into the ground. Tie a 1-foot rope through each of the tarp holes onto three sides of the tarp. Tie a peg or stick onto each rope. Pulling the tarp tight, pound each of the pegs firmly into the ground.

Good Idea *Pitch your tent in an open area where the first early morning sun will quickly dry off any dew that collected during the night.*

Stay Safe *Tents and fire don't mix. The tent should be far enough away from a campfire that wind-blown sparks can't reach it.*

Log or Boulder Tent

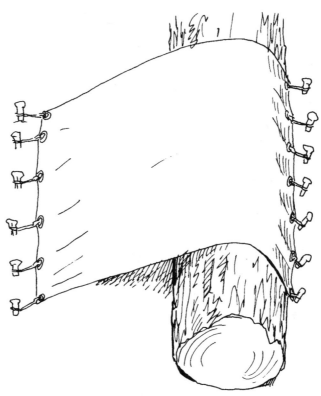

Tie a 1-foot piece of rope through tarp holes on one side of the tarp. Tie a tent peg or sturdy stick onto each free end of these ropes. Place the tarp over the rock or log, and pound each peg into the ground. Pull the tarp over the rock or log. Tie short pieces of rope onto all the tarp holes on the opposite side of the tarp. Attach tent pegs or sturdy short sticks to these ropes. Pull the tarp tightly across and over the boulder or log. Pound each of the pegs firmly into the ground.

Make Your Own Rope

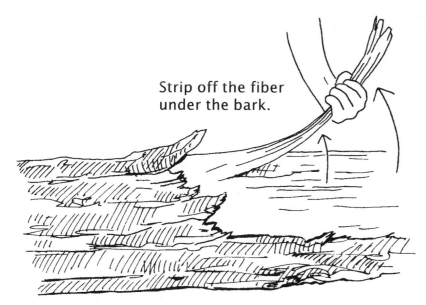

Strip off the fiber under the bark.

MATERIALS

Dead tree
Water

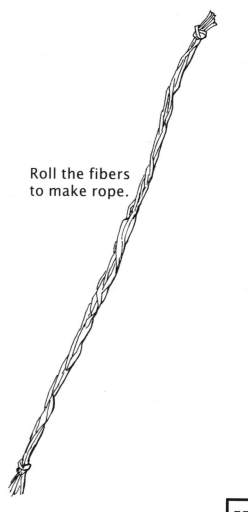

Roll the fibers to make rope.

Find a dead tree lying on the ground. (If you strip bark from a live tree, you may kill it.) The best trees will have the bark already rotting off. Pull the bark off to find the stringy fiber directly beneath the bark. You will be able to easily pull the fiber off the tree with your hands.

Wet the fibers and roll them between your hands or against your leg. Rolling will make the fibers softer and easier to work with.

After the fibers are soft and pliable, twist the fibers together lengthwise until they begin to kink. Hold the middle of the rope firmly beneath one foot and put the two ends together. Pull firmly. This will make the rope twist together naturally when you let go of it. Tie each end into a knot to secure your rope.

You can make many sections of rope and tie them together to make a really long piece.

Tie Some Knots

MATERIALS

Long shoelaces
Cotton or nylon rope

 Tying knots is a necessary skill for camping. You will use knots to tie up a clothesline, set up a tarp-tent, tie your gear together, and many other projects around the campsite. Once you learn the art of knot-tying you will never forget how to tie knots.

Practice tying knots until you are quick and the knots are strong and sturdy. When you are just beginning to learn knot-tying, it is easier to practice on long shoelaces. After you can easily tie the knots with shoelaces, practice with rope.

Overhand Knot

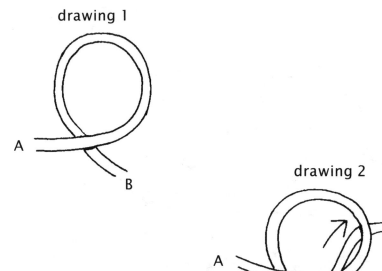

drawing 1

drawing 2

 This is a simple knot to learn first. This knot is tied with one rope. Lay your rope on a table or flat surface. Bring the right end of the rope around and over the left end of the rope, forming a circle (drawing 1). Bring the left end over the right where it forms the bottom of the circle. Then bring the left end in and under the circle on the right side. Firmly pull both ends to tie the knot (drawing 2).

Square Knot

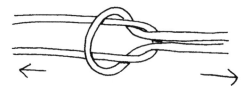

Pull the ends to tighten.

The square knot is used to tie two ropes together and will not slip even when it is pulled hard. Make a loop in the middle of each rope. Place one of the loops facing right and the other facing left. Place the right-hand loop over the left hand loop. With your fingers in the bottom loop, pull the rope ends of the top loop into and through the bottom loop. Pull firmly on both sets of rope ends to complete your knot.

Overhand Loop

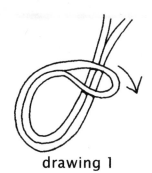

drawing 1

drawing 2

This is another knot that uses only one rope. It is made with a doubled rope that makes a stronger knot than the overhand knot. Fold the rope in half forming a loop. Form a circle by bringing the loop around and over the rest of the rope (drawing 1). Take the loop behind the bottom of the circle, up and through the circle (drawing 2). Pull firmly.

Bowline Knot

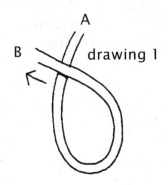

A

B

drawing 1

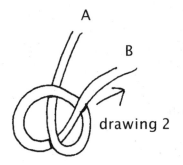

A

B

drawing 2

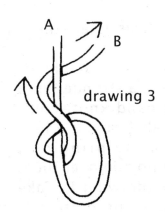

A

B

drawing 3

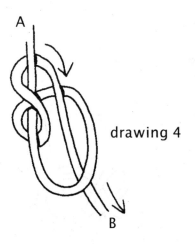

A

B

drawing 4

 This knot is a little harder to learn than the first three knots, but it is well worth the effort. The bowline knot is great for hanging things (such as your food), and setting up the tarp or tent. You use only one rope.

Form a loop in the rope by bringing one end up and over the rope (drawing 1). Form a second loop by bringing the end of the rope behind the bottom of the loop, into the loop, and over the top of the loop (drawing 2). Pass the end around the back and up the part of the rope above the loop (drawing 3). Bring the end down over the top of the loop, and then through and behind it (drawing 4). Pull firmly to set your knot.

Hang a Clothesline

U se your new skill at knot-tying to hang a clothesline you can put your wet clothing and towels on. You don't even need clothespins to hang stuff on this one!

MATERIALS

2 cotton or nylon ropes

Tie one end of both ropes together with an overhand knot. Twist the ropes together until you reach the other end of them. Tie the second end with an overhand knot also.

Locate two trees that are close enough to each other to reach with the clothesline. Tie the clothesline onto each tree using a bowline knot.

To hang your clothing on this clothesline, tuck the corners of the clothing between the twists in the rope.

Make a Broom

MATERIALS

Bunch of sturdy grass
3-foot stick or branch
3-foot length of heavy cord or thin rope
Scissors

✺ Find some thick, sturdy grass. Cut the grass off near the ground and gather it into a bundle the size you would like your broom to be. Find a straight stick or branch for the handle. Don't cut it from a tree or bush; look on the ground for limbs that have already fallen off the tree.

Place the bundle of grass near the bottom of the stick so that the stick is about halfway up the length of grass.

Make a fold about ¼ up the rope. Lay the fold at the point where you would like to attach the grass to the stick. Be sure to keep the ropes parallel to each other.

Beginning 2 inches from the bottom of the short portion of the rope, wrap the long portion of the rope around the handle and the grass. Continue wrapping with the long rope until 2 inches of the top fold are showing. Push the end of the rope through the loop. Pull on the lower rope end. This will pull the rope end under the wrapping and secure the rope around the broom. Trim the rope ends.

Branch Broom

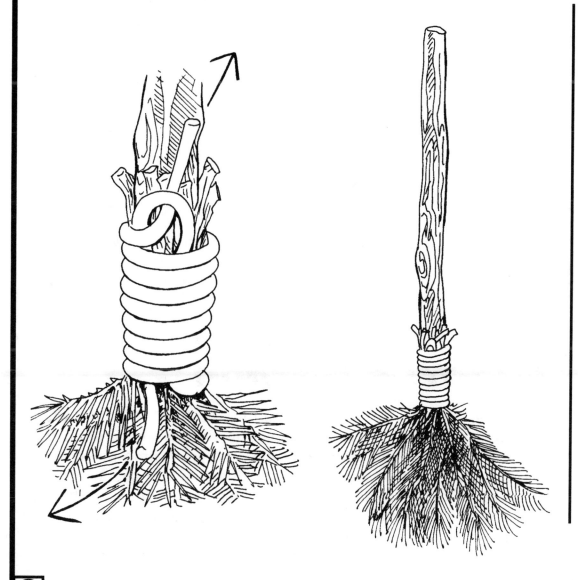

MATERIALS

Four 2-foot pine branches
3-foot stick or branch
4-foot length of lightweight rope

Look for the branches and the stick on the ground rather than pulling them off a living tree. Place the end of the branches near the end of the stick. Fold 1 foot of the rope down so that it forms an upside-down "U" and is parallel to the rest of the rope. Place the "U" over the branches and the stick. Take the rope and wind it around the branches, stick, and the ropes.

Continue wrapping in an upwards direction until about 2 inches of the loop remains unwrapped. Insert the free end of the rope into the loop. Carefully pull the rope end at the bottom down. This will pull the free end of the rope into the wrappings.

Tie It High

MATERIALS

Pillowcase, sleeping bag sack, pack, or duffel bag
Nylon rope
Small rock

Hang your food from 2 trees like this.

Wild animals love the taste of people food and don't know it isn't healthy for them. If you can't store your food in a vehicle at night, hang it in a tree. This way, the animals will eat the food in nature that's best for them.

There are two ways to hang your food from trees. Be sure the food bag hangs at least 15 feet off the ground so that an animal can't reach it when standing on its back legs.

Gather your food, medicines, toothpaste, and dishes and put them into a strong pillowcase, stuff sack from your sleeping bag, pack, or duffel. Tie a 40-foot nylon rope onto the opening of the food bag. Tie a small rock onto the other end of the rope.

Two-Tree Method

Find 2 trees with heights of about 18 feet. Have an adult climb the first tree with a rope and tie one end around the tree. Bringing the free end of the rope with you, climb the second tree, and tie the rope around it. Standing beneath the stretched rope, toss the rock (tied to the rope that holds your food bag) over, and pull on the rope until the food bag won't go any higher. Wrap the rope around a tree trunk and tie tightly. When you need to get to your supplies, untie the rope and lower the bag to the ground.

One-Tree Method

Hang your food from 1 tree like this.

 Look for a large, strong tree with a strong branch high on the tree that sticks out about 10 feet from the tree's trunk. Throw the rock with the rope tied to it over the end of the branch. Pull on the end of the rope until the food bag is just below the branch. Wrap the end of the rope around the tree's trunk and tie tightly.

To get your supplies, untie and lower the bag to the ground.

NATURAL WONDERS

After you've set up camp, it's time to explore! See what you can discover using more than just your eyes. *Listen* for the sounds of nature, such as buzzing insects, roaring rapids, and the whistle of wind through the treetops. *Sniff* the smells of the outdoors: fresh pine needles, sweet-scented wildflowers, or salty breezes off the ocean. Use your body to get in *touch* with the velvety squish of mud between your bare toes, the slippery-slick surface of a fish, and the warm sun on your skin. Don't miss a thing!

While you're camping, you'll notice things you didn't pay attention to before. You'll be able to see how all of nature works together. Watch the clouds full of rain overhead and the sun's rising and setting. Look for animal tracks hinting of their search for food or homes.

While camping, *you* are part of it all! It's a great time to notice everything—perhaps you'll discover something you've never seen or thought about before.

Make a Sun Clock

MATERIALS

Straight stick
Rocks
Wristwatch

If you would like to tell time the way it was done before watches were invented, try your hand at making a simple sun clock. You will need a watch to use when you are marking the time—then put it away for the rest of your stay, and use the sun clock instead!

Find a straight stick and push it into the dirt in a sunny place. Every hour, place a rock where the stick's shadow ends.

At noon the stick will cast no shadow, as the sun is straight overhead. One side of the stick will be shaded in the morning hours and the other side in the afternoon hours. When you have finished, your rocks should end up in a straight line.

> **Nature Note** Is this old saying always correct?
>
> *"Red sky at night, campers delight,*
>
> *Red sky in morning, campers take warning!"*

Mark the stick's shadow every hour with a rock. Use it to tell the time tomorrow.

Weather Watching

When you're in the out-doors, weather takes on a special importance. Your tent may be the only shelter from a drenching rainstorm, all-day drizzle, or even a snowstorm! Learn to watch the clouds for telltale signs of what weather changes will be arriving soon.

cumulus clouds

If you know what the weather might be doing, you can plan the best times for hiking, and the best time for staying in the tent and doing a craft project. That way, a storm won't ruin your trip. Plan some crafts, like weaving a basket, to do inside the tent during a rainy spell. When it's over, have a sketchbook ready to record the beautiful rainbow over the lake! Make the most of every minute you're in the great outdoors.

Watch for weather signs in the sky overhead. While not every cloud will bring a storm, it's best to beware of the different types of clouds and what they could be bringing your way. *Cumulus* clouds are easy to spot in the summer sky. They look like giant cotton balls. If they are small, it means the weather will stay nice except for the chance of a few scattered showers. If they combine into larger and larger clouds and turn dark, you may get rain, lightning, and possibly hail. Keep an eye on those large cumulus clouds. The longer it takes for them to turn dark, the longer the storm will last.

When you see *cirrocumulus, cirrostratus,* or *altocumulus* clouds, it may mean rain within 24 hours or less. These clouds are usually higher in the sky than cumulus clouds. Cirrocumulus clouds look like miniature cumulus clouds gathered together high in the sky. Cirrostratus clouds are ice clouds that are generally straight in shape and are thin, which allows the sun to shine through them. Altocumulus clouds are small cumulus clouds in rows parallel to each other. These clouds generally mean a longer storm than the cumulus clouds.

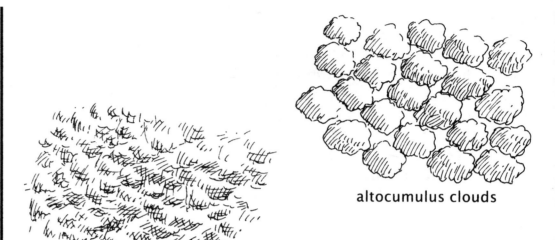

altocumulus clouds

cirrocumulus clouds

cirrostratus clouds

Cloud Diary

Want to keep a "Cloud Diary"? Take along a bag of cotton balls, white glue, and a spiral notebook. Each day, record the date and make a note of the time. Then stretch the cotton balls into the cloud shapes you see in the sky above you. Glue them to the page with dots of glue. Label them with their cloud name. Record any other weather happenings in the diary, too.

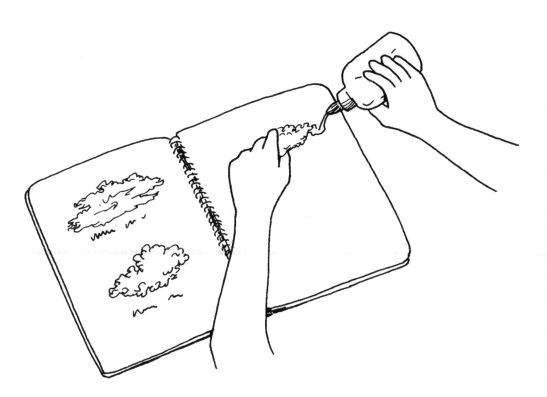

MATERIALS

Cotton balls
White glue
Notebook

Nature Note *Years ago before television and radio weather reports, people made sayings to help predict the weather. While they don't always come true, note in your cloud diary if there is dew or not. Then later in the day, record the weather. How often does this old saying come true?*

"When dew is on the grass, rain will never come to pass. When morning grass is dry, look for rain in the sky!"

Nature Note *Find the direction of the wind by wetting your finger and holding it up in the air. The side that feels coldest is the direction the wind is coming from.*

Record Some Sounds

MATERIALS

Tape recorder

Nature Note *To hear better in the wild, cup both ears forward with your hands. This creates large ears like a deer or other large-eared creature. You will not only hear what your ears are pointing to but that sound will be louder. Turn around in a circle to hear all the sounds.*

Take along a tape recorder and record a souvenir of your trip. Here are some sounds to listen for:

Birds chirping and singing
Water gurgling, roaring, and splashing
Insects singing
Frogs croaking
Wind whistling through the trees
Coyotes howling
Owls hooting in the quiet hours before dawn
Parents snoring—even the clatter of dishwashing!

You can record the sounds alone, or record a sound and then tell what it was on the tape. You can also say where you heard it and the date or time of day it was heard.

While hiking, you can record your feelings. Is the hike easy or difficult? How does that drink and snack taste? What did you feel when you first saw the lake, cliff, waterfall, or wild animal? When you're back home, it's easy to forget what you felt and saw when you were camping. The tape could become a very interesting "diary" of your vacation—fun to listen to on a rainy winter day. The sounds you make while camping are important, too. Noisy campers scare away the wildlife and irritate neighboring campers.

Use a tape recorder to capture the sounds of the outdoors.

Watch for Wildlife

When you are in the wild, you may come upon a small trail made by animals called a game trail. You won't see any piled rock markers or blazes on trees to mark the way. It will be time well-spent to follow this trail, keeping watch for animal signs. The most obvious sign to look for will be tracks and scat (animal waste droppings). Watch for tree-scratching, branches and grass chewed by animals, homes of small rodents and birds, hair left on branches, and deer or elk beds.

Tree scratches can be made by mice, members of the cat family, or bears. Look at how high the scratches are, and the size of the scratches. The smallest and lowest would belong to the rodent family, then would come the cat family, and last and highest would be made by a bear.

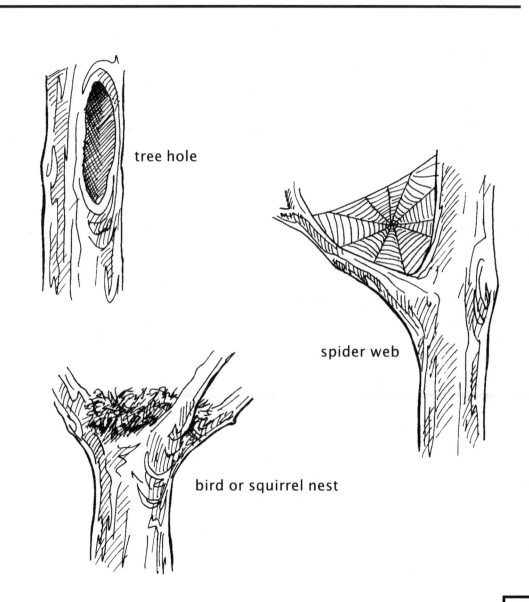

tree hole

spider web

bird or squirrel nest

If you spot a "scratching tree," look around the tree for pieces of fur or hair, as these trees are also used as a back-rubbing post. If you spot a tree missing large amounts of bark in an oblong shape, this could be a mark made by a porcupine. Porcupines eat tree bark. If the nibbled patch is above your head, it wasn't a huge porcupine—just one that stood on deep snow to nibble bark.

tree scratches

Nature Note *If you find a baby animal or bird, leave it alone. Don't touch it or move it. The mother is probably right in the area or has left the baby there for safekeeping. Many animals will not want their baby to smell like a human. Your smell can also attract predators to the baby.*

porcupine gnaw

How to Find Animal Homes

Homes for some animals and birds can be easy to find, and, for other animals, almost impossible. Some of the easiest to find are bird and squirrel nests, or burrows in the ground. To find nests of birds or squirrels, look up in the tree branches or in old, hollow trees.

Chipmunks, snakes, ground squirrels, foxes, badgers, coyotes, prairie dogs, and lizards all live underground in burrows. To find if a hole in the ground is occupied, stick a few small twigs upright in front of the hole. Leave the area and return later to check on the twigs. If they are flattened or bent, it means that some creature has been using the hole. Sit quietly at a distance and watch. You may spot the hole's dweller as it enters or leaves the burrow.

To find a deer or elk bed, look for a flattened area of grass, usually under a tree. The area may contain piles of scat that looks like large rabbit droppings. If you spot one of the flattened grass areas, look around for hair left in the area, or shrubs and grasses that the animal has been chewing.

> **Nature Note** *If you are watching an animal and its ears start twitching and it is looking at you, it is becoming scared. Stay where you are and you may be able to watch it. Go no farther! It may run off in fear or try to defend itself. Wild animals can be unpredictable.*

Beavers leave very clear signs of their presence in the forest. Trees they have chewed down leave a unique stump. This stump will end in a sharp point with piles of wood chips around the ground. Beavers don't build dams with large trees. These trees are stored in the water for their winter food. Beavers eat the bark off these trees during the winter.

Beavers build their homes in free-flowing rivers or streams. They build dams by laying small trees across a stream until it creates a pond. They build lodges in the pond out of round piles of sticks. If you spot one of these large piles of sticks in a pond, look around for the beaver's woodlot and try to spot some of the pointed stumps.

If the beaver has built a pond you can easily spot the dam. They build it from branches and mud. Don't walk on their dam, as you can damage it, and fall through into the water.

If you are lucky and find a beaver pond in a marshy area, look for tiny channels of water in and among the grasses. These are the beavers' "highway." The beavers will swim in these lanes as they travel around the area.

beaver stump

beaver lodge

Watching for Birds

Birds are very interesting to watch in the wild. Some birds live year-round in the same area, other birds fly thousands of miles each year as they migrate between their summer and winter homes. Birds live in the mountains, deserts, plains, meadows, and even in towns and cities. They are among the few wild creatures that we see everyday.

They eat fruit, seeds, fish, insects, and nectar; some even eat rotting meat. Birds such as the pheasant do very little flying, while some birds, such as the eagle, fly long distances at great heights searching for their meal.

When you are bird-watching, notice how each kind of bird is different from the others. A peacock is very different from a hummingbird. The hummingbird beak is long, thin, and sharp while the peacock has a long, beautiful tail. Why? The hummingbird's beak helps it to reach nectar in flowers and if it had the peacock's tail it wouldn't be able to hover over the flowers and would soon starve to death. As you watch birds, try to figure out what each bird eats by the shape of its bill and feet.

The bills on birds are made for the type of food that they eat. Seed-eating birds have short, thick bills that they use for crushing seeds. The insect-eating birds have slender, pointed beaks for picking up insects. Birds that kill and eat meat have strong bills with sharp, curved hooks that they use to tear the meat apart.

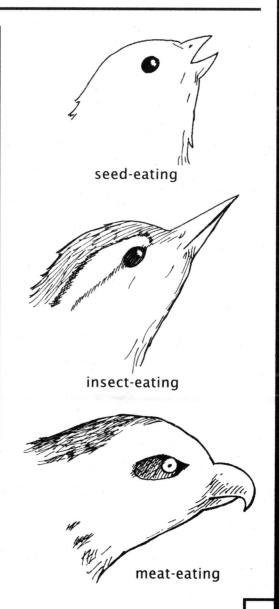

seed-eating

insect-eating

meat-eating

There are two types of birds that eat on or near the water. The duck or goose has a wide, flat bill that it uses to strain its food from the mud and water. Birds that catch fish, such as herons, have sharp, pointed bills that they use to spear fish and frogs.

bill for straining mud

bill for spearing fish

Birds perch, wade, scratch, swim, climb, and hunt with their feet. Perching feet are the most common feet you will see. Birds use perching feet to hold onto branches and wires. Ducks and geese have a different type of feet for swimming. Their feet, which are big and broad with skin between the toes, act as paddles in the water. Birds that spear fish have a large foot with three long, skinny toes. These feet help the bird to stand and wade in mud without sinking. Look at the eagle on a dollar bill and notice his feet. Birds of prey such as the eagle, hawk, and owl have this kind of foot. Their feet are very strong and sharp with curved talons that grip and hold onto the bird's prey.

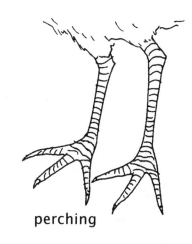

perching

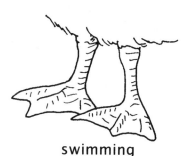

swimming

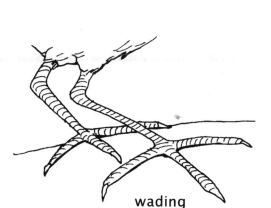

wading

gripping prey

Birds build many different types of nests. Some nest on the ground, some on ledges, some on water, and some in trees. Learn to recognize a good nesting site and stand quietly. If you are lucky, you may glimpse a mother or father bird bringing food home to the babies.

Here's an easy way to bring birds up close for viewing. Fill some bowls with food attractive to birds. Try unsalted seeds such as sunflower or sesame seeds and fresh berries. Even though you may have seen people feed bread to birds, it's best for the birds if you stick to seeds and berries. Bread is delicious to birds, but it's like us eating candy all day—you're stomach feels full, but you haven't eaten the healthy foods you need.

Sit quietly and watch from a short distance away. Watch to find out which birds eat at dawn, during the day, and at dusk; which birds prefer seeds and which prefer berries; which bird is the shyest and which feed in flocks. As you watch, look for differences in birds. What do the beaks look like on different birds? How do they differ among the seed and berry eaters? Which bird is the largest and which is smallest? Which colors do you see the most in the birds? How are their feet different?

If you have your journal with you, record how many of each species come to eat, what time of day they visit and which food each type of bird prefers to eat. This is also a great time to make drawings of the birds in your sketchbook!

Grow a Bird Nest

MATERIALS

1 camp bowl (see page 15)
Bird nest

Find an abandoned bird nest. Search the nest and the area below it for broken bits of eggshell. If you find eggshell, the young have already hatched and flown away and won't be needing the nest anymore. Place the bird nest in the camp bowl with ¼ inch of water on the bottom of the bowl. Add more water when needed to keep the level about ¼ inch deep.

In a few days all the seeds that were left in the nest by the birds will start to grow. Wait and watch to find out what seeds were fed to the baby birds.

Find an empty bird's nest.

Put it in a pan of water and watch for sprouts.

Mysterious Owl Pellets

MATERIALS

Tweezers
Toothpicks
Magnifying glass

When you are on a hike you may find a gray, fuzzy lump under a tree or cactus. This could be an owl pellet. When owls eat their food, they usually eat it whole or in large chunks—bones and all. The bones and fur are then spit up in the form of pellets.

Look for owl pellets.

To examine the pellets, you should carefully remove all the bones from the fur ball and try to figure out what little animal the owl had for dinner. Use a pair of tweezers and toothpicks to pick the pellet apart. A magnifying glass will help you examine the tiny bones and teeth in the pellet.

Look for owl pellets at the base of a tree or cactus where an owl is nesting. Look around the area for a hole in the ground, if it is a burrowing owl. You can spot the owl's home and return at dusk and watch from a distance. You may catch a glimpse of the owl as it goes about the nightly business of hunting for its dinner!

Who Made That Track?

MATERIALS

Make a "Track Trap" so you can capture some animal footprints.

Bowls and pans
Broom (see page 60)

 Walk around your campsite and collect natural foods for the animals and birds. You will need a bowl or pan for each type of food. Some foods to look for are berries, grass seeds, pinecones, nuts from nearby trees and flower seeds.

Find an area which is muddy or filled with loose soil. Place the bowls around the area and sweep away all prints with your broom. Leave and return later. You may want to wait overnight because many animals feed at night.

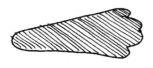

rabbit

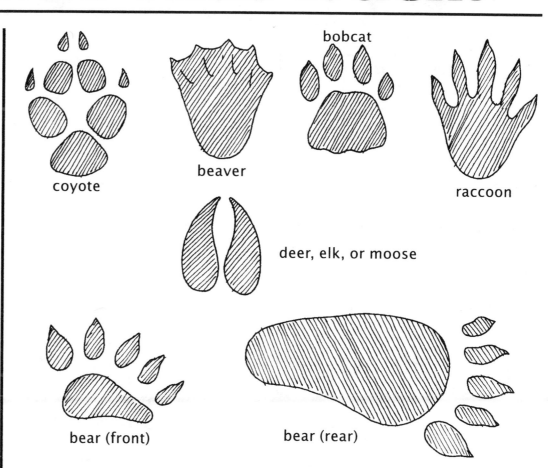

coyote

beaver

bobcat

raccoon

deer, elk, or moose

bear (front)

bear (rear)

Check the dirt or mud for tracks before you walk onto it. If you find some, try to identify the bird or animal that made the track. Check the bowls to see which food was eaten. You will learn which food animals like to eat best.

If no animals have come to eat, you may want to experiment with different foods. Use only natural foods that grow in the area because people's food can be harmful to animals.

Take Some Tracks

MATERIALS

Plaster of paris
Water
Can, or plastic jug
with top cut off
Spoon or stick for mixing

Follow the directions on the package for mixing the plaster and water. When it begins to thicken (about 10 minutes), pour it over a track and let it harden.

In about an hour, gently lift the hard plaster and carefully brush away the dirt. You have a copy of the animal's footprint to take home!

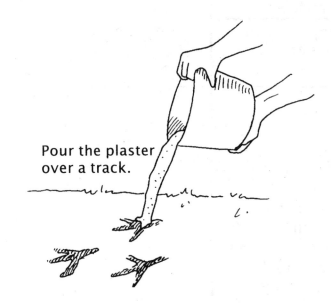

Pour the plaster over a track.

Stir plaster and water until it starts to thicken.

When it hardens, brush off the dirt and take home a track!

Make a Bug Net

MATERIALS

Wire coat hanger,
or willow branch and duct tape
Nylon stockings
Scissors
Needle and thread

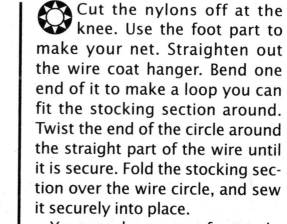

Cut the nylons off at the knee. Use the foot part to make your net. Straighten out the wire coat hanger. Bend one end of it to make a loop you can fit the stocking section around. Twist the end of the circle around the straight part of the wire until it is secure. Fold the stocking section over the wire circle, and sew it securely into place.

You now have a net for catching bugs or fish. If you are observing water creatures, be sure to keep the net in the water as you watch them. Release all the creatures after you are done studying them.

No coat hanger at camp? Use a long, flexible willow branch. Roll the end back to make a loop and secure it with duct tape. Fold the nylon stocking over the hoop and stitch with a needle and thread.

Cut the leg from some nylons.

Bend a wire coat hanger or willow branch to shape. Twist the wire or tape the branch with duct tape.

Fold the stocking edge over the hoop and stitch with needle and thread.

Insect Hunt

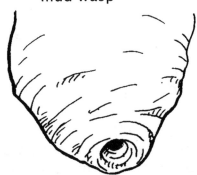

mud wasp

While you are out hiking, watch for insect homes. If you are looking carefully, you may spot the small, round indentation in the ground that marks a trap-door spider's home.

Look for small amounts of bubbles on grass stems. These are homes for small insects sometimes called "spitbugs" or "spittlebugs." Can you guess why? These insects suck the juice from plants to make a frothy ball to hide in that looks a little like bubbly spit.

Wasps and hornets make nests that are easy to spot. These can hang on bushes or along the roof eaves of a building. If you spot one of these hives, be sure to observe from a distance because wasps and hornets can sting you severely.

Can you spot a spider's web? Follow a honeybee home to the hive? Locate an anthill on the forest floor? There are many living creatures, right under your feet!

paper wasp

Soil Sifting

MATERIALS

Soil sifting screen (see page 31)
Small garden trowel
Empty egg carton
Glue
Marker
Field guide to rocks and minerals

Nature Note *Magnets are fun! Take some along and move them over different types of dirt to see how much iron is in it.*

Sift soil through the screen.

Before you dig, make sure you have permission and that digging is allowed. Creeks and riverbanks are good places to begin looking for rocks as many types of rocks wash down the creek in the springtime when melting snows fill the streams. The rocks are carried along in the rushing water and are left along the banks.

Scoop some dirt or gravel onto the screen and sift the dirt through the holes. To sift, rub your hand gently back and forth over the dirt. It will fall through and the rocks will stay on the screen. Examine each rock to see if you like it enough to keep it. Sometimes dirt will cover the rock so you will need to rub the dirt off or wash it to determine what it looks like.

After you have collected your samples, you can glue them in the empty egg carton. Label each one with the date you found it, where you found it, and what it is called. Check a field guide if you're not sure what kind of rock it is (see page 170).

When you finish, fill in all the holes you dug.

Rock Collection

Glue rocks in egg cartons. Label them with their name and when and where you found them.

Use egg cartons to sort and display your rocks. With glue or a tacky adhesive compound (like Sticky-tack), attach a stone in each egg section. Write the name of the rock (use a field guide to help you learn the names) on a piece of paper and glue it next to the stone. You can enjoy quite a large collection if you stack the closed cartons on a shelf or in a closet.

MATERIALS

Egg cartons
Clear nail polish
Paper
Glue or a tacky adhesive compound (like Sticky-tack)
Marker
Field guide to rocks and minerals

Watch the ground, and you're bound to find some interesting rocks and geologic specimens.

When you get home, give your stones a coat of clear nail polish to make them glisten, just like the shiny ones in a stream bed!

Be a Dirt Detective

Collect dirt samples from different areas near your campsite, and save them in boxes or pans. While you are gathering the samples, look at the plants growing in each area. You don't need to take a large sample—a few shovels full of dirt will be enough.

Sift the dirt through the screen and examine it. How does it smell? What bugs live in the soil? How many and what types of plants and roots are you able to identify? How much earth, rock, or sand is in each sample? How many pine needles or decaying leaves? From your observations, try to learn which soil is able to grow the most plant materials. What soil receives the least amount of water, and how does that affect the soil? Which is the most friendly environment for insect life? What soil smells the best to you? The least pleasant? Why?

When we visit an area, we sometimes think of the dirt as being the same in the whole area. By being a Dirt Detective, you will find that this is not always true. Soil by a creek will often be very sandy and unable to support a large amount of plant life, while the soil just a few feet away contains a large insect population and many roots from grasses and flowers.

The soil under a large, towering tree often does not support any plant life because of the shade and acidity of the soil caused by fallen and decaying leaves or needles.

The soil under a fallen tree only supports plants which need a great deal of shade. These plants could include the fern, which reproduces by spores on the back of the leaf. Use your magnifying glass to find these spores. Use your magnifying glass to find these spores. At first, they are tiny green spots. Later in the season, they will turn dark when they are ready to fall off the plant. On the

MATERIALS

Soil sifting screen (see page 31)
Trowel
Boxes or pans
Magnifying glass
Typing paper
Outdoor journal (see page 26)

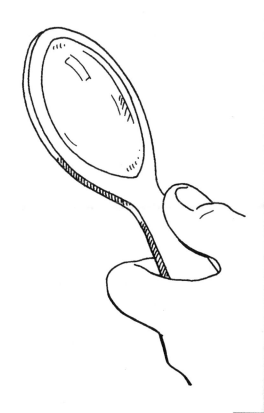

ground, they will grow into new ferns. Gently shake a fern leaf over a piece of paper. Ripe spores will fall onto the paper. If they don't, gently pry them off the leaf with your fingernails. Look closely at them through your magnifying glass; how do they look?

If you are in a wet, wooded area in the spring, look for the Lady Slipper. It looks like a wild orchid only a few inches high. These plants are quite hard to find, so if you are lucky enough to see one, don't pick it but sketch it instead in your journal.

Soil in an open grassy area often contains a large amount of root material. Identify the insects living in the roots if you have a field guide along. If not, draw a picture so you can look it up later. Look for insects along the stems of plants and in the seeds and flowers. What insects does each soil support?

By being a Dirt Detective, you will learn a lot about the natural world all around you. Look for miniature worlds in the area. Which soil is most like a desert? Which soil is grassy and rich? Which is like that in jungles or rain forests?

We usually look around us and notice the large things. We see the trees, but not each blade of grass. We notice the deer, but not the tiny beetles. While looking at a lake, we don't notice the tiny ant search for its way around a puddle. Watch an anthill. Does it remind you of a busy city of people hurrying about their work? Sit quietly and watch an insect. Does it crawl through dew or go around? Dig up an earthworm. What does it do next? Look for dead insects. Study them with a magnifying lens. Draw pictures of them in your journal. You may want to begin an insect collection. You can use a field guide to learn more about the insects you see.

> ***Nature Note*** *Many plants and flowers "grow by the inch and die by the foot." Walk around plants instead of stepping on them, if you can.*

Press Some Plants

Collecting Plants

Wherever you go in the outdoors, there will be interesting plants. You can select a few to press and dry to keep them for a long time. When collecting plants, be sure you are in an area where it is permitted.

Snip or break the stems, leaving the roots in the soil to grow new plants. Also leave a few flowers so that the plant can create seeds for next year's plants.

Look for unusual plants: delicate ferns, mosses, interesting grasses, tiny flowers, and water plants. Take along an old telephone book or thick magazine. Position each plant you find between the pages separately. Close the book or magazine, and, when you get home, place something heavy on top of it. This will flatten the plants as they dry. Drying takes a week or two.

MATERIALS

Cardboard (2 pieces)
Newspaper (10 pieces)
Waxed paper (20 pieces)
Belt or large, heavy rubber band
Scissors

 Cut the cardboard, newspaper, and waxed paper into squares about 1 by 1 foot. Lay down one piece of cardboard, 1 piece of newspaper, 2 pieces of waxed paper, 1 piece of newspaper, 2 pieces of waxed paper, 1 piece of newspaper, and then 2 pieces of waxed paper. Continue this stacking pattern until you have used all the newspaper and waxed paper. Lay the other piece of cardboard on top. Buckle the belt around the middle of the cardboard so that it fits snugly, or use a large, heavy-duty rubber band.

Plant Press

If you want to make a plant press at home to take along on your camping trip, here's how to do it.

Layers of cardboard, newspaper, and waxed paper hold flowers and plants for pressing. Fasten it with a belt or thick rubber band.

When you find a plant, flower, or leaf that you would like to preserve, put it in the press between 2 pieces of the waxed paper. Buckle the belt snugly after each addition. The plants should be pressed for about 1 week; then, they're ready for you to use.

Pressed Plant Crafts

MATERIALS

Colored paper
Clear adhesive plastic
Mat board
Photo album
Glue
Scissors
Marker

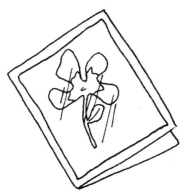

Make beautiful cards.

Glue pressed flowers to colored paper. Cover with clear adhesive plastic.

After your plants are dry, take them out of the press and glue them to colored paper to make cards or displays. Use your pressed plants to decorate holiday and birthday cards for special friends and relatives.

Cover the plants with a piece of clear adhesive plastic. You can glue several dried plants to a piece of mat board and frame it to give you a year-round reminder of your walk in the wild!

Pressed plants can be used for any number of craft projects. Use your pressed flowers and some glue and colored paper to make collages, greeting cards, and placemats.

Make a botanical collection by gluing samples in a photo album. Label each dried plant with its name and where you found it. Use a field guide to find information about each plant (see page 170).

Nature Note *When you are collecting anything outdoors, be sure that you have the landowner's permission or that it's allowed where you are camping. Many areas, such as national or state parks, have very strict laws forbidding the collecting of anything.*

Always cut your plant or flower above the ground with scissors so that the root is not damaged and will produce more plants and flowers. Do not pick flowers unless you are able to count at least 20 of the same kind nearby. For pressing leaves, you can find many different kinds lying about on the ground.

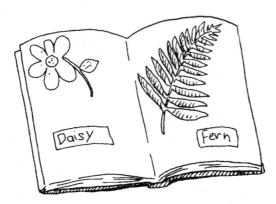

Make a collection of pressed plant samples in a photo album. Label each one.

A Treasure Hunt

MATERIALS

A small prize
Paper
Pen or pencil

Write a set of directions telling someone else how to find a hidden treasure. For example: "Start at the picnic table, and take 15 steps west to the tree stump. Go north until you come to the blue flowers. Turn to the left and go 14 paces to the pine tree. Look under the pile of leaves behind it."

Take turns hiding the treasure, and following the directions to find it!

Take a Sock Hop!

MATERIALS

Old socks
Clear tape
Large envelopes

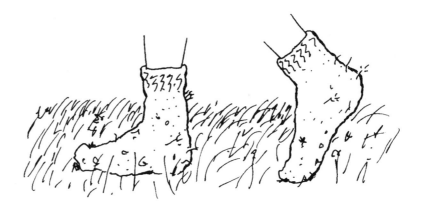

Put some old socks on over your shoes and take a walk through a meadow or other grassy area.

Return to camp and pick off all the seeds and burrs that have collected on your "seedy" socks. Separate the seeds into groups. Go back to the meadow and try to identify which plants the seeds came from. If you have a plant field guide, you can read about each type of plant. Learn what the plant's name is, where it grows, and what the plant's flower looks like.

Use some clear tape to tape a few seeds to a page of your outdoor journal and write down the facts next to the seeds. Save a few seeds in a sealed envelope to take home and plant in a garden or flowerpot.

CAMP CRAFTS

W hile you're out in nature, you will be inspired by the beauty around you. The sights and sounds of the wild will get your creative juices flowing. If it's a little rainy or cold outside, this is the best time to stay inside and work on some crafts. You can use different objects that you find around your campsite—pinecones, pine needles, leaves, acorns, pebbles, and twigs. Let your imagination be your guide.

When you're getting ready to go camping, make a list of the things that you will need to pack with you to do these projects. You just won't find some of these materials, such as paper, crayons, paint, and glue, out in the woods.

Twig Sculptures

MATERIALS

Paper plate
Twigs
White glue

 Collect twigs of different shapes and sizes. When you have as many as you think you need, start to make your sculpture. Use the paper plate as a base. Position the twigs on top of each other, gluing them together as you go to make an interesting structure. Break the twigs to the size you need as you work. You may have to hold them in position for a few seconds until the glue sticks.

You can make a sculpture of anything you like—make it look like something real or create a unique design. Continue adding to and building the sculpture until *you* think you are finished.

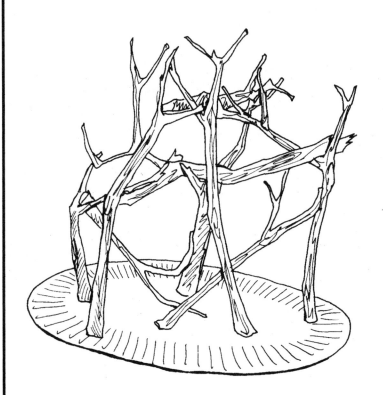

Glue twigs on a paper plate to make a sculpture.

Twiggie Creatures

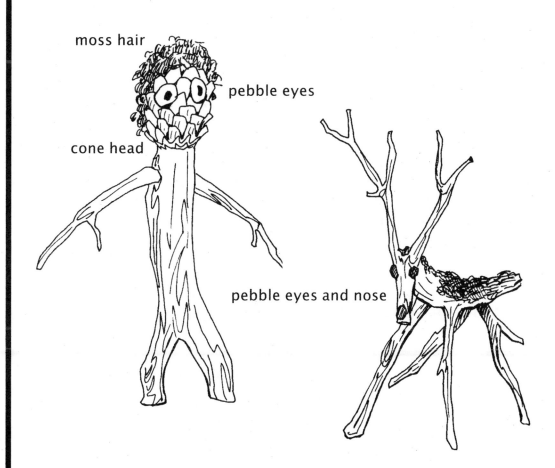

moss hair

pebble eyes

cone head

pebble eyes and nose

Glue twigs together to make creatures.
Add moss, pinecones, and pebbles for details.

MATERIALS

Twigs, moss, pine needles, and bark
Small white pebbles or beans
White glue
Fine-tipped black marker

Gather together some twigs, moss, pine needles, and bark. Now it's time to create a Twiggie, a truly unusual creature. Think of how you want your Twiggie to look.

Break the twigs to fit the shape that you decide on. Then, glue the pieces together. Use the marker to draw in black dots to make the white pebbles look like eyes. Glue them in place for eyes. When your Twiggie is finished, you can brush a coat of glue over it to give it a shiny look when it dries.

Give your Twiggie hair made of dry moss, or make a reindeer with twig antlers to use as a decoration next Christmas. No two Twiggies are exactly alike!

Little Log Cabins

MATERIALS

6-inch twigs
Paper plate or piece of cardboard
Craft glue
Heavy paper or cardboard
Grass, moss, bark, pebbles,
and acorns (optional)

Gather some twigs and make a tiny cabin like the ones that pioneers made from logs long ago—except yours will be much smaller.

Make sure that your twigs are all about 6 inches long and not too crooked. Lay two twigs across from each other about 5 inches apart on a paper plate. Lay two more across them to make a square. Glue them together where they touch, and squirt glue under them so they are attached to the plate. Position 4 more twigs on top in the same way, gluing them as you go.

Lay 4 twigs on the paper plate. Glue in place. Glue on layers of twigs to build the cabin.

Fold cardboard to make a roof.

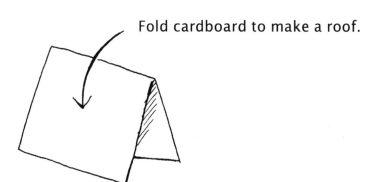

Continue building up the cabin walls until they are as tall as you want. Cut out a rectangle of heavy paper or cardboard to make a roof. Fold it down the center in the shape of a "V." Glue it on top. If you want, you can glue on bits of dry grass to make it look like a thatched roof. Or you can glue tiny chunks of bark onto the roof to look like shingles.

Look for small pebbles for a fireplace or path, and bits of dry moss for bushes. Also collect tiny twigs and acorns, and glue them together to make little people for your cabin!

Glue stones for a fireplace.
Use moss, pebbles, and twigs for details.

Twig Basket

You can find willow branches growing on shrubs along creek banks or lying beneath willow trees. If you can't get any, look for other types of long, sturdy branches that you can bend in half without breaking. Be sure to get permission before you cut twigs from living trees or bushes.

Keep the twigs moist in a bucket of water (or a plastic jug with the top cut off) because they bend easier when they are wet.

Lay 8 of these one way, and the other 8 crosswise to form a "+" shape. These 16 twigs will form the foundation of the basket.

Take a new twig and make 3 rounds weaving over and under these groups of 8. Go over 8 twigs, then under 8, then over 8, and so on until you have made 3 rounds.

MATERIALS

Twigs that bend easily,
such as willow
Bucket or plastic milk jug
Water

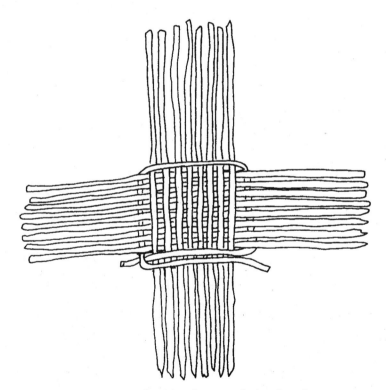

16 twigs make the base of the basket.

Separate the twigs into pairs of 2 twigs and weave around them, going over and under, to make 3 complete rounds. Now weave over and under the twigs one at a time. Continue the over-under pattern to make the rest of the basket.

When the twig you are using to weave with starts getting short, add a new one to it and weave them together for a few turns. Drop the old one and continue weaving with the new one. You can add new base twigs the same way.

To make the sides of the basket, bend the base twigs up while you are weaving. Start the sides when the bottom of the basket is as wide as you want it.

To end the basket, tuck the base twigs back and down into the woven part. If ends come loose, you can use a hot-glue gun when you get home to secure them.

You can also make a basket like this from long grasses, cattail leaves, or reeds—anything flexible that can be woven.

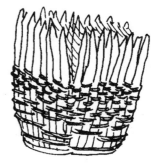

Weave the sides.

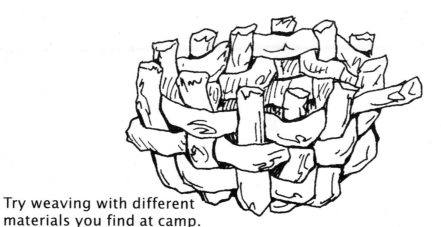

Try weaving with different materials you find at camp.

Tiny Twig Raft

Layer and glue twigs on both sides. Let them dry.

MATERIALS

Twigs (or popsicle sticks)
Waterproof craft glue

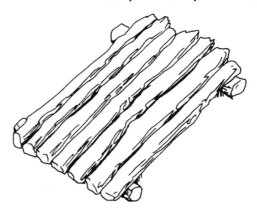

Make sure you collect twigs that are all the same size and length. If you can't find enough of them, use popsicle sticks.

Lay down two twigs for the ends. Glue twigs on top of them. When the glue is dry, turn the raft over and glue another layer of twigs crosswise.

Let the glue dry completely before putting it in the water. If you want to be sure it doesn't float away, tie a long string to it so you can pull it back to shore.

Pine Needle Necklace

You can make bracelets, necklaces, and even decorative belts using pine needles that you collect.

MATERIALS

Pine needles

cap

Make a chain of pine needles to wear around your wrist or neck.

Find some pine needles that are growing in bundles of two to five leaves. The bundles of leaves are gathered at one end with a thin cap; this cap attached the leaves to the tree.

Pull all but one of the needles out of the cap, being careful not to pull the cap off. Bend and push the end of the needle back into the cap, making a loop. This will be the first loop in a chain. Repeat for more loops, but link them through the last loop you made before you push the needle's tip into the cap.

When your chain is as long as you want, insert the last needle through the first loop before you push it into the cap.

Pine Needle Basket

ine needles are an evergreen tree's leaves. They keep their leaves all year round, but some drop off during the summer while new ones grow. You can gather piles of old needles from the base of a pine tree.

MATERIALS

Long, dry pine needles
Bucket of water
Scissors
Yarn or heavy-duty thread, and
yarn needle
Plastic drinking straw

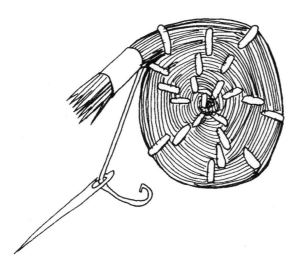

Find some pine needles, the longer the better, lying at the base of a pine tree. Before beginning, soak the needles in water for about 30 minutes because wet needles are easier to shape.

Thread the needle with about 2 feet of yarn. You can knot the end and tie on new lengths of yarn as you need it.

Cut off a 1-inch length of the drinking straw. Fill it with enough pine needles to fit easily, but not loosely, inside it. Wrap the end of the yarn around the end of the pine needles until they are secure. Bend the pine needles into a round coil. With needle and yarn, stitch the coil onto the coil next to it about every ½ inch.

Continue adding more pine needles as you use them up. When you add them, just slide them into the straw, and work them into the coil.

Continue coiling and stitching until the base of the basket is as big as you want it. As you go around the basket, lay the coil on top of the last round of the basket to shape the sides. Continue around the basket laying each new coil above the last until the sides of the basket are the size you want. Continue coiling and stitching the ones left in the straw until you run out of pine needles. Make 3 stitches in the same spot, and tie off with a tight knot.

To preserve your basket and make it look shiny, coat it with acrylic floor wax or spray acrylic finish when you get home.

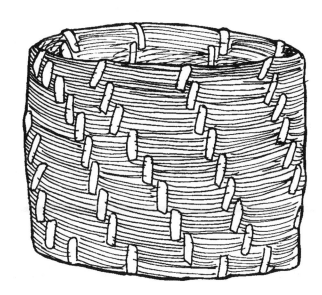

Pinecone Turkey

Aren't pinecones fascinating? They grow on many evergreen trees besides pine. From tiny alder cones to large sugar pinecones, each type of tree carries its seeds in a different shape of cone. Check the cones before you gather them. If the petals have spread open, look between them to see if seeds are still in the cone. Take home only cones that have lost their seeds. Leave seed-bearing cones and those with petals still closed for squirrels and chipmunks to eat or for starting new trees next spring.

MATERIALS

Pinecone
Brown construction paper
Feathers
Brown pipe cleaner
Scissors
Red marker or crayon
Glue

Cut a head and neck from brown paper, and color a wattle below the bird's beak with a red marker. Fold the end and glue it to the base of the pinecone.

Glue the feathers in between the cone petals to create a tail.

Pull the pipe cleaner down firmly around the pinecone's center, hiding it between the cone's petals. Pull it tight and it will stay in place. Curve the ends to create two feet.

You can also use a walnut or peanut for the turkey's head, securing it with a hot-glue gun (with grown-up help). Color on the eyes with a marker. Glue a bit of red felt or a colored paper cutout for the wattle.

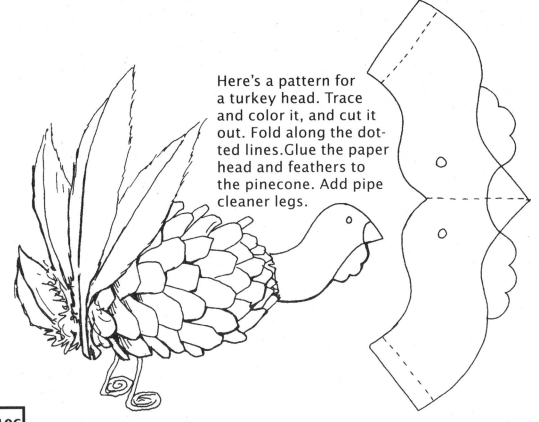

Here's a pattern for a turkey head. Trace and color it, and cut it out. Fold along the dotted lines. Glue the paper head and feathers to the pinecone. Add pipe cleaner legs.

Pinecone Trees

While you're hiking around, collect the different shapes and sizes of cones you see. Why not gather some to take home for craft projects this winter? Cones keep for a long time, so save your extra ones in a box in the garage or attic.

Since cones come in such a wide variety of sizes and shapes, your cones may help you decide what projects you want to do. Look at your pinecones carefully and see what ideas spring into your mind.

MATERIALS

Pinecone
Green or white tempera paint
Glitter
Paintbrush
Newspaper

This is super easy, and you'll love the results.

Working on a table covered with newspaper, paint the pinecone green. Make sure you brush inside the petals of the cone so that it's completely covered with paint. Before it dries, sprinkle glitter onto the wet paint.

Instead of green paint, you can paint the edges of the cone petals with white paint, creating a snowy effect. Sprinkle on glitter before the paint dries. Try other colors, too. Paint your pinecone silver and sprinkle with red glitter.

Make a forest of these little trees. They look pretty clustered in a bowl on a table or set at each place setting for a table decoration or party favor.

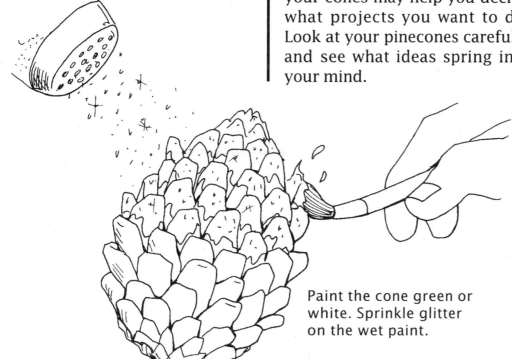

Paint the cone green or white. Sprinkle glitter on the wet paint.

Cattail Leaf Mat

MATERIALS

Cattails
Scissors
Clear plastic shipping tape

Make a mat to sit on or use as a placemat at the picnic table. You will find cattails growing in wet areas or along the banks of ponds. Get permission to harvest a few for this project.

After you get permission, cut down a large bundle of cattail leaves close to the ground using scissors. Lay the leaves side by side until they are as wide as you want the mat to be.

Insert a leaf crosswise to the others, weaving over a leaf, under the next, over, under, over...continue this pattern until your mat is as long as you want.

Be sure to straighten the leaves and push them together tightly as you work so you won't have loose spots or spaces in the mat.

When it's as large as you want, trim the edges with the scissors. Press half the width of the tape around all four edges on the top of the mat. Fold the other half of the tape over and press it firmly to the other side of the mat. The tape will keep it from coming apart.

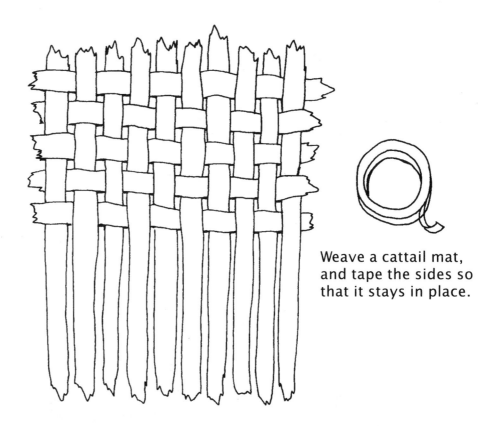

Weave a cattail mat, and tape the sides so that it stays in place.

Leaf Stencils

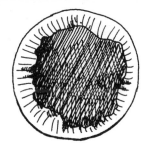

Sponge paint around the leaf's edges.

MATERIALS

Leaves
Tempera paint
2-by-2-inch sponge pieces
Paper
Newspaper
Paper plate

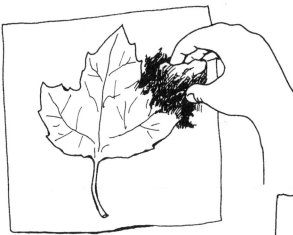

Lift the leaf and you'll see its outline stenciled in paint.

Lay newspaper down so that you don't get paint on your work surface. On top of the newspaper, place the paper on which you want to print, and put the leaf on top of that. Squirt some paint onto the paper plate and dip the sponge in it. Gently dab paint around the edges of the leaf onto the paper.

When you've done the whole leaf, carefully lift it up, and you'll see it's shape outlined on the paper. Try all sorts of different colors because leaves come in different colors.

Leaf Splatter Painting

MATERIALS

Leaf
Paper
Cardboard
Newspaper
Straight pins
Tempera paint
Paper plate
Old toothbrush
Stick

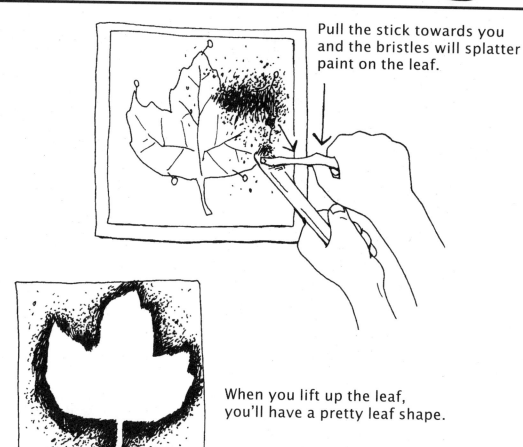

Pull the stick towards you and the bristles will splatter paint on the leaf.

When you lift up the leaf, you'll have a pretty leaf shape.

Lay down some newspapers. You might also want to wear an old shirt that you don't mind getting a little paint on.

Cut a square of cardboard from a box; make it slightly larger than the sheet of paper that you want to paint on.

Place the paper on top of the cardboard and carefully position the leaf on the paper. Use the straight pins to hold the leaf in place around the edges.

Squirt some paint onto the plate. Dip the toothbrush into the paint and pull the stick across the bristles *toward* you to splatter paint onto the leaf and paper. Splatter on different colors, if you want. When it's dry, unpin and lift the leaf and take a look at your painting.

Leaf Rubbings

Rub the paper with crayons to make a colorful leaf pattern.

MATERIALS

Leaves, grasses, weeds, and fern fronds

White paper

Crayons

Newspaper

Layer the newspapers on the tabletop to pad the surface. The rubbings will look better with plenty of padding underneath. Place the leaves and weeds on top of the newspaper and lay the white paper on top.

Peel the paper wrapping from the crayons, and rub them over the paper, using the sides instead of the pointed ends. Press firmly and the outlines and the veins and ribs of the leaf will show through. Change positions of the leaves, and change colors of crayon as well.

Use the paper for placemats at the picnic table, or for gift wrap, note cards, and book covers when you get home.

Fish Printing

MATERIALS

A fresh, flat fish,
such as trout, perch, or bass

Newsprint or shelf paper
for printing on

Colored ink or acrylic paints

Soapy water

Paper towels

Newspapers

Brayer for spreading ink or paint

Look closely at the fish—it's a work of art itself! The beautiful scales, curved gills, and feathery tail are worth saving as a work of art. Fish are colored differently to help camouflage them in their environment so that predators can't see them. Some fish can even change their coloring for better protection! You can mix paint colors to match the color of your fish, or make it any color—even a rainbow!

Spread ink over the fish.

If you'll be camping near a lake or stream, you may want to try fishing. Check with the local Fish and Game Department. They will tell you what type of fish can be caught, how many are allowed, and what kind of bait to use. Ask for a copy of the fishing regulations; it will have drawings of fish to identify your catch.

You can use one of your catch to print with. If you don't catch any, you can always get a small fish at the grocery store.

Cover the inked fish with paper and press down to print out a fish pattern.

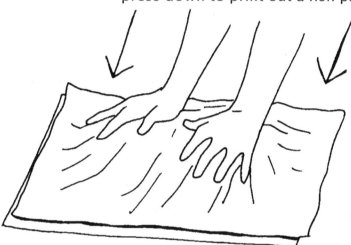

Wash and dry the fish gently with soapy water and paper towels. Place the fish on the newspaper, making sure that the tail and fins lie flat.

Use a brayer to roll ink or paint over the fish, moving from head to tail to keep the scales smooth. If you don't have one, use your hands. When the fish is completely covered, lay a piece of paper for printing on top of the fish. Press over the fins to be sure they print, too.

Lift up the paper and you'll be surprised to see how the details of the fish were captured.

You can print the same fish several times, adding more paint or ink when needed. If the scales get too filled with ink you can rinse the ink off with water, dry the fish with a towel, then re-ink it, perhaps with a different color. You may want to print some seaweed or grasses, so your fish will appear to be swimming in its natural habitat.

Paper Folding

MATERIALS

Paper from an old telephone book, magazine pages, or newspapers, typing paper, or gift wrap

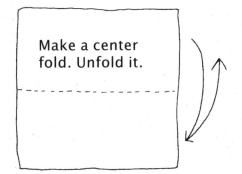

Make a center fold. Unfold it.

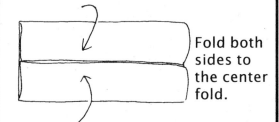

Fold both sides to the center fold.

Turn over. Fold the corners to the center fold.

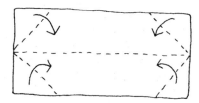

Origami is the ancient art of folding paper into shapes. It was invented in Japan, where the word *origami* means "paper folding." Take along some papers to use at camp; this is a perfect thing to do in your tent if a light rain begins to fall.

You will need squares of paper to fold. A good size to work with is 4 by 4 inches, but 6- or 8-inch squares are good, too. You can make yours larger if you wish, as long as it is a square—all sides are the same size.

Follow the instructions with the illustrations to fold your creations.

Fold in half.

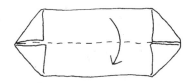

Turn over and open, pressing the boat into shape with your fingers.

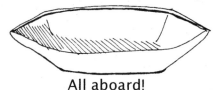

All aboard!

Floating Boat

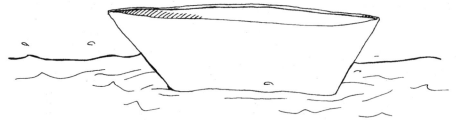

The floating boat works best if you put a tiny acorn or pebble in it to weight it evenly, so it won't lean to one side.

Swimming Duck

Take your folded swimming duck and boat along in your pocket to use at a pond or lake.

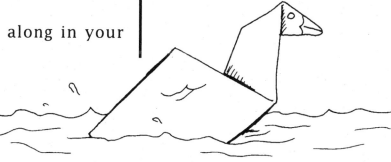

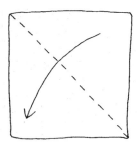

Make a diagonal, center fold. Unfold it.

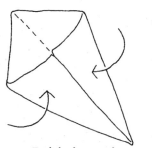

Fold the sides to the center fold.

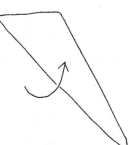

Fold in half.

top view

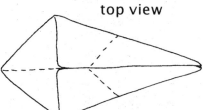

Fold back the long end, tucking it inside the body.

side view

Fold down the end again to make a head.

MATERIALS

Newspaper

 Use old newspapers to fold a fun hat to wear anytime.

You can wear it on your head, or turn it upside-down and use it to hold flowers, leaves, or tiny pebbles you find on your walk.

Fold a Hat to Wear

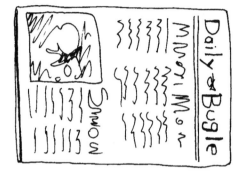

Fold the top corners of the newspaper to the center, and crease.

Fold up a brim around the bottom. Crease it so that it stays in place.

FUN & GAMES

Camping out gives you a chance to leave your usual toys, games, and sports behind while you enjoy new ways to have fun outdoors. Be sure to take along sporting equipment that might be fun depending upon where you will be camping: swim fins, snorkels, fishing equipment, hiking sticks, softballs and bats, or Frisbees. They can make the outdoors more fun—if you have room to take them along. Here are some easy-to-do camp activities that don't take a lot of equipment or supplies.

Make a Golf Course

MATERIALS

Toy golf clubs, curved sticks, or clubs made from rolled-up newspaper and tape

Golf ball or small ball

Empty soup cans

9 paper cups

Nine 12-inch sticks

Marker

Spoon for digging

Can opener

Make a golf club out of newspaper and tape.

Bury cans in holes in the ground and them number them with paper cups hung on sticks.

Make a can tunnel for the ball to go through.

If you don't have a toy golf club, try and find a curved stick lying around the campsite that will work. You can also make a club by rolling up some newspaper in the shape of a club and taping it in place.

Look for an open area away from where people are camping or fishing. An open meadow or beach is perfect. Set up your course with nine holes, one following another. Ask the camp cook to save some soup cans for you to use in your holes. Use the spoon to dig a hole large enough to fit the can in. Place a can in the ground so that the ball can roll in.

Turn the paper cups upside down and write numbers from 1 to 9 on each. Hang each one on a stick stuck in the ground near each of the holes.

Cut the ends out of a can that you can use as a tiny tunnel that the ball must pass through before getting to the hole.

To play, take turns hitting the ball into the holes, starting with hole #1 and going in order to #9.

Super Soap Bubbles

MATERIALS

6-foot length of string
2 plastic drinking straws
Dishwashing liquid
(Joy brand works well)
Water
Glycerin (from the drugstore)
Tiny safety pin
(that fits inside a straw)
Shallow pan
More bubble wand ideas:
wire hanger and duct tape, or
plastic container lids

Tie one end of the string to the tiny safety pin, and drop it through both straws. Take off the pin and knot the ends of the string together, making a large loop. This is your bubble wand.

Mix several tablespoons of dishwashing liquid with a bit of water in the shallow pan. You may have to add more water or soap to get just-right bubbles. Add a few drops of glycerin to make the bubbles last longer.

Have you ever made some really big soap bubbles? Well, camping out gives you just the right setting for making some whoppers! Take along the supplies, but remember not to get the soap in freshwater streams or lakes because it can harm the plants and animals.

Make the bubbles by holding the straws in your hands and dipping the straws and string into the soap. Lift it out and hold your hands apart while waving the mixture through the air to create a huge bubble.

You can also make a wand out of thin wire or an old coat hanger. Twist it into the shape you want; use duct tape or masking tape to hold the ends together. Dip the loop end into the soapy mixture and wave it through the air to make bunches of bubbles!

To make a round bubble wand, use scissors to cut away the rim from a lid of a plastic container, such as the ones whipped topping or yogurt come in.

Make your own bubble wands from everyday items: straws and string, the lid from a plastic container, or a piece of wire.

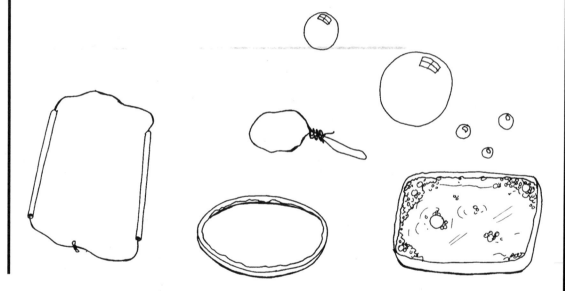

Simple Sailboat

MATERIALS

Plastic bottle or jug
Stick
Cloth or paper scraps
Clay
Scissors
Glue
Nail and string (optional)

 Cut the bottom part away from a plastic bottle. Press a ball of clay into the bottom of the boat and push a stick into it for a mast. Add a cloth or paper flag.

If you want to keep it from floating away, work a hole in the side with a nail and tie on a long length of string to pull your boat back to shore.

Cut out the bottom of a plastic bottle.

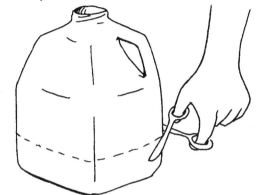

Cut out cloth or paper flags.

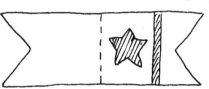

glue

Glue the flags to a stick mast.

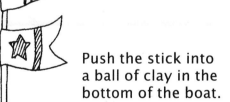

Push the stick into a ball of clay in the bottom of the boat.

Tie a string to pull the boat back to shore.

Fly a Kite

MATERIALS

Lengths of willow or thin branches, or ¼-inch dowels

Ball of string

Newspaper or large sheet of tissue paper

Scraps of lightweight cloth

Knife (with grown-up help)

Scissors

Glue

Hint *It's easier to feed out string quickly while the kite is flying if you wind the ball of string around a cardboard tube. You can then put a 12-inch stick through the tube and hold the ends of the stick while the string rolls out quickly and smoothly.*

Camping is the perfect time to fly a kite—no overhead power lines to worry about! If you're camping near a desert or a beach where there are no trees to get the kite caught in, it's a great idea.

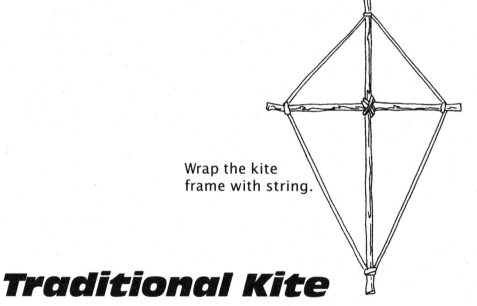

Wrap the kite frame with string.

Traditional Kite

To make a good kite, you need to keep the length and width in proportion: the length must be ⅓ more than the width. Good sizes are 15 inches long and 10 inches wide, or 36 inches long and 24 inches wide.

Tie two sticks together tightly with string in the shape of a cross. You may have to flatten the area where they meet, using a knife. Ask a grown-up to help with the knife.

Make notches about 1 inch from the ends of each stick. Wrap string around the ends of the sticks, winding it once around at each notch. Knot it securely.

Lay this frame on the newspaper and cut the paper in the same shape, but make it 1 inch larger all around. Cut out "V" shapes around the notches on the ends of the sticks. Fold the edges of the paper down over the string and glue them to hold.

Cut a length of string about 6 inches longer than the longer stick. Tie it to the top and bottom of the stick at the notches.

Tie the end of the ball of string to this string at the center of the kite.

Dab a bit of glue on all knots and notch areas to strengthen them.

Cut or tear about 10 strips of lightweight cloth and tie them to a 12-foot length of string. This is the kite's tail, and it will keep it stable in the wind. Tie it on at the bottom notch.

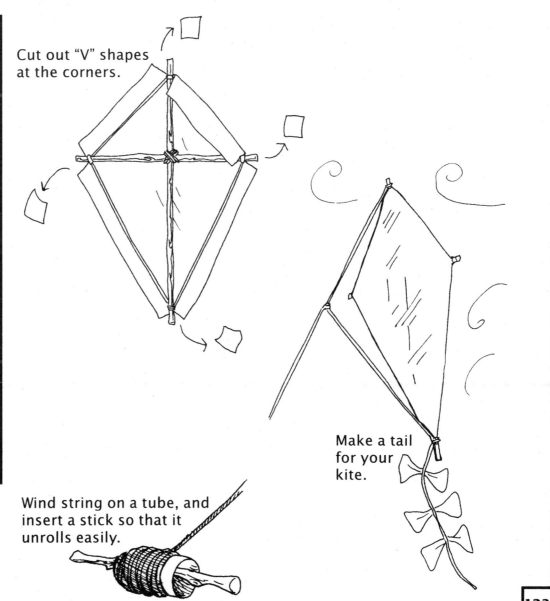

Cut out "V" shapes at the corners.

Make a tail for your kite.

Wind string on a tube, and insert a stick so that it unrolls easily.

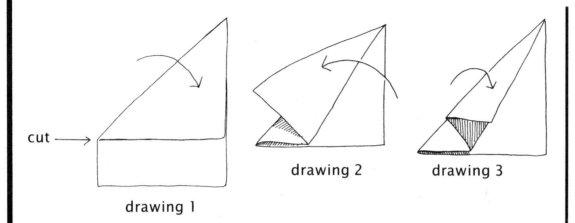

cut →

drawing 1

drawing 2

drawing 3

MATERIALS

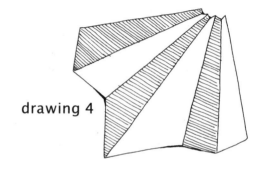

8½-by-11-inch sheet of paper
Spool of thread
Small stick or pencil
Scissors
Tape
Hole punch

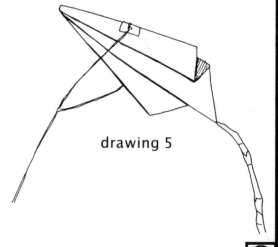

drawing 4

drawing 5

Fold a Paper Kite

Fold the top edge of the paper over along the side to make a tri-angle-shaped corner. Crease the fold and cut off the extra paper on the bottom (drawing 1). Fold both sections of the paper up and then down again, like an accordian (see drawings 2 and 3). Snip off a small amount of the point (drawing 4).

Cut the leftover paper into six strips the same size and tape them together lengthwise to make the tail.

Tape the tail to the middle crease at the end of the kite. Mark a point about two-thirds of the way down from the tip of the kite on each outer edge. Reinforce these with tape and punch a hole at each mark.

Cut a length of thread about 2 feet long and tie an end into each of the holes. Attach the spool of thread onto the middle of this loop (drawing 5).

Insert a small stick into the thread spool for handles.

Frog & Flies

 Choose one person to be the Frog, the rest are Flies. Pick a spot to be the "Base," away from the circle. To play, the Frog squats in the center of the circle and the Flies go around him in the circle until the Frog jumps up and chases the Flies. Any Flies tagged by the Frog before they get to Base become Frogs and help tag Flies during the next round. The last Fly to be tagged becomes Frog for the next game.

Bird, Fish, or Beast

Play this game with a group of people. One person is "IT" and the rest should get in a circle around him or her. IT points to a player and says, "Bird," or "Fish" or "Beast." The player must answer with the name of one of these types of creatures. For instance if the person who is IT says "Fish," the person he or she pointed to might say "Trout," which is a type of fish. If the player is correct, he becomes IT. Don't use any creature name more than once.

Nature Knowledge

MATERIALS

Paper
Pencil

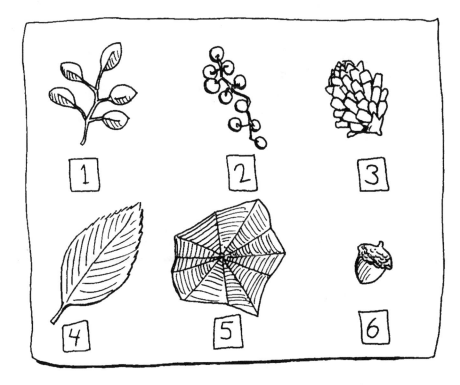

Number each of the items. Players write down their answers.

This game can be played by all ages. Let the younger children simply name the item, and expect older players to be a bit more specific. Your little sister may only be able to tell the difference between a pebble and a shell, while you may be able to tell the difference between a piece of quartz and a chunk of fool's gold (iron pyrite). After all the guessing is over, use field guides to make sure the answers are correct.

Choose one person to organize the game. This person collects between 5 and 20 different objects from around the campground. Some ideas are plants, flowers, berries, leaves, pebbles, twigs, or shells.

Number each object, and then give each player a turn identifying the objects. Give everyone a notepad so that they can write down the number and what they think the object is. After everyone has made their guesses, compare the answers.

Track Memory

MATERIALS

Field guide
Paper or cardstock
Scissors
Pencil

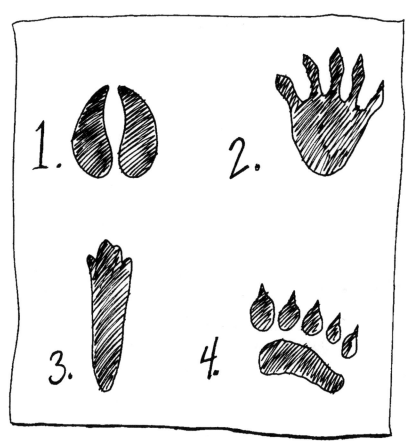

Cut the paper or cardstock into pieces the size of playing cards. Draw animal tracks on the pieces of paper. Use a field guide to find out what the tracks should look like. If you want, make more than one of the same track.

Lay the papers in a stack, face down like a deck of cards. Take turns picking a "card" off the top of the stack and naming the animal that made the track. If you answer correctly, keep the card with the track you identified. If not, put the paper under the stack and let the next player take a turn. You can keep score, or just play for fun. If there are questions about the tracks, be sure to look them up in the guide.

Guess whose tracks these are.

Scavenger Hunt

MATERIALS

Pencil
Paper

When you find something that's on your hunting list, write down where you found it.

One player makes a list of 20 easy-to-find things. Some good ideas are leaves, twigs, flowers, feathers, insects, berries, seeds, pinecones, rocks—anything you have around camp.

Divide up into pairs or teams of players. Give each team a list, and send them out to search for as many items as they can find within a certain time limit. A grown-up should go with each team to be sure no one gets lost.

Don't take the items away from where you found them. Pick someone from each team to make a list of what items were seen and where they were found. When you get back to camp, compare what each team found.

Predator & Prey

 One player is the Predator, the rest are the Prey. While the Predator covers her eyes and counts to 20, the Prey run and hide. The Predator opens her eyes after reaching the number 20, and any Prey that she sees and points to are "out." The Predator closes her eyes and counts again, and the Prey players try to sneak past her. If she hears a noise and points to them, they are "out." Any Prey that sneak past the Predator without being pointed to are "safe." The last person to be "out" is the Predator for the next round.

Can Toss

Empty cans

Balls, pinecones, nuts, stones, or acorns

Marker

Paper

Tape

Tape numbers on empty cans. Toss pebbles or pinecones.

Ask the camp cook to save you some empty food cans. Remove the labels and tape a paper number to each one. Set them up and mark a line about 10 feet away. Stand behind the line and toss small balls, pinecones, nuts or stones into the cans. If you toss one into a can, add the number on the can to your score. You can play with others, or just keep trying to beat your own score.

TAKE A HIKE

There are many types of trails in the wild. The trails can range from trails that are kept clean of fallen logs and plant growth to trails that animals, such as mountain goats, sheep, deer, or elk make in their travels. In general, stay on the trails made and maintained by people, as you might get lost if you follow the animal trails. Learn how to read a map and how to follow trail signs and markers. Always hike with an adult and stay together while hiking.

If you think you may be lost while hiking it is important to stay where you are and wait for help! You will feel frightened and want to try to find your own way out. But if you stay where you are, people will have a good idea about where to search for you. It is possible to run miles off the trail if you are panicked.

Whenever you are hiking it is always a very good idea to carry a loud whistle with you. Blow on this whistle 3 loud, short bursts and then wait for a few minutes before you repeat the 3 bursts again. Keep blowing this way as long as you can as this is a recognized "Help" signal. The whistle will carry farther than your voice will and will not tire you out as much as shouting will. This whistle should always be with you for emergencies and must never be used for play.

To be able to hike for a long distance you will find that the best speed is slow and steady. Many people try to hurry and go as fast as they can. When you hike too fast you will get tired very quickly. Keep a snack bag in your tote or pack and munch on this as you hike. Good snacks to take along are: dried fruit, such as raisins or fruit leather, jerky or some salty snack, such as peanuts or chips, candies to suck on, granola bars, and some chocolate. For some recipes for take-along food, go to the "Fix Some Food" section of the "Get Ready, Get Set...Pack Up!" chapter on page 35. Take your water bottle along because it's important to drink plenty of water as you hike. You will use up a lot of your body water and if it is not replaced you will become very tired and even sick.

It's important to take a rest now and then. This is a good opportunity to explore a nice spot you've noticed along your hike. If you are very tired and your legs are hurting, your first thought will be to sit down. But if you sit down too much while resting your muscles could tense up making it much harder to hike after your rest. For this reason it is a good idea to remove your tote or backpack and rest standing up.

Feet can get very sweaty while walking and socks can rub your feet, making painful blisters. When you come to a stream or water take off your shoes and socks and cool your feet in the water. Spread your shoes and socks in the sun to dry out. Check your feet carefully for blisters. If you find that you have a blister or one is starting to develop you must treat it then and there. You should have some moleskin "donuts" along in your first-aid kit. (See the Pocket First-Aid Kit in the "Get Ready, Get Set...Pack Up!" chapter, page 28.) Clean the blister with water, dry it, and press the moleskin donut around the blister. Then place a bandage on top of the moleskin.

While you are hiking it is important to protect your face and eyes. In sunny weather wear a hat or visor to shade your face from the sun. It will protect you from heat exhaustion and sunburn. *Use sunscreen on every part of your body exposed to the sun.* It's a good idea to wear sunglasses, too.

When you have decided which trail, how far you will hike, and who is to go with you and have gathered your snack bag, water bottle, first-aid kit, sunglasses, hat, and raincoat, it is time to hit the trail! While you hike, keep your eyes open for animals and plants. You will find that hiking is great fun and you will find many interesting things on your travels. Enjoy!

Good Idea *While hiking, be polite and let faster hikers pass you. Move out of the way for horses and heavily loaded backpackers.*

Stay Safe *Wear a whistle on a cord around your neck. If you're lost or have an accident, blow hard 3 times to call your family.*

Mark Your Own Trail

At times, you will not have a clear trail to follow no matter how well-maintained the trail is because of fast-growing plants, rocky ground, sections of fallen trees, or other debris. It is wise to learn the trail signs and markers that are known the world over. These markers are used on grasslands, rocky ground and woodlands. You will not find any trail markers on animal trails.

One of the most common trail markers is the *blaze*. Blazes will be found on trees along most trails. This mark is made by chopping off bark in an oval shape and a small circular shape directly above the oval. This mark helps you to follow the trail when it is covered by plants or snow or hard to find. Blazes are made by the trail workers who build and maintain the trail.

> ***Caution*** *If you decide that you would like to make your own trail, you must always have a knowledgeable adult along on the hike. Along with the adult, be sure to take a topographical or "topog" map of the area. A topog map shows the features of the area by the use of lines on the map. Each line stands for a different altitude. When you know how to read a topog map, you can tell where the cliffs, meadows, mountain slopes, rock slides, lakes, springs, and canyons are.*

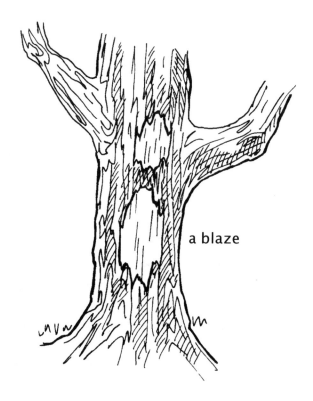

a blaze

Another common marker is the *cairn* built with stones. Cairns are found where the ground is rocky and a trail would be hard to build and maintain. By knowing and following these trail markers, you will be able to follow the trail even when you can't see a well-worn path.

Blazes and cairns, along with grass and stick markers, can tell you when to go straight, turn left, or turn right; when you are facing the wrong way; and when to get help. Grass and stick markers are not used often, but they are used sometimes when the grass grows rapidly and the trail crew is not able to keep the trail cleared.

By knowing these markers, you will be able to mark your way through an area without using a trail. This way, you can follow them back and return to your starting point.

> **Nature Note** While hiking on a trail that zigzags uphill or downhill, stay on the trail. If you take shortcuts, you can harm plants and soil, and cause erosion after a rain.
>
> **Stay Safe** Be sure to drink lots of water in warm weather. If it's hot, drink even when you're not thirsty. Your body loses moisture through the skin faster in hot weather.

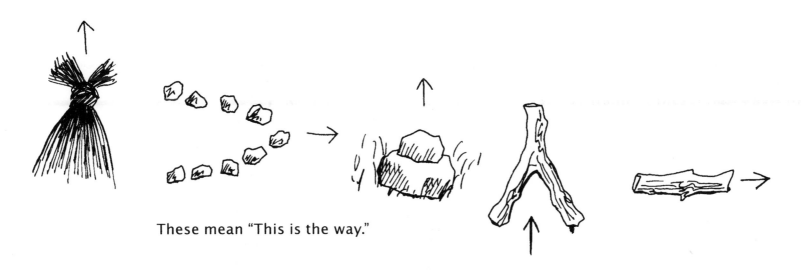

These mean "This is the way."

These mean "Turn right."

These mean "Turn left."

These mean "Not the right way."

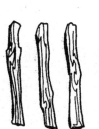

These mean "Danger—Help!"

Map It Out

You can draw a map for any area. Make a map of the campground, marking where the tent, bathrooms, lake, trail, water, bushes, trees, and roads are.

Make your own special map of a hike you went on. Mark down what is of special interest to you. Show where you saw the deer, bird, spring, picnic spot, or anything else you choose. Draw it as detailed as you like. Color it in with markers.

Here are some activities you can do with maps.

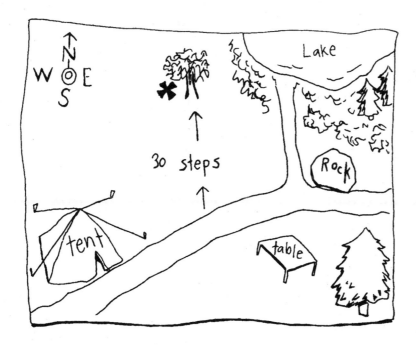

MATERIALS

Coin
Paper
Pencil

Trail Flip

Take a coin, paper, pencil, and a grown-up out for a hike. Every 5 minutes flip the coin to see if you go left or right. Make a map of your hike so you can find your way back again. This is a good time to try your hand at marking a trail (see page 136).

MATERIALS

Paper
Marking pens

Follow That Trail

 Have a grown-up go out before your hike and make a trail using trail markers (see page 136). Follow the markers and make a map of the hike as you go. Return by following the map and trail markers.

MATERIALS

A prize, such as foil-wrapped coins, gum, or a can of soda
Paper
Marking pens

Go on a Treasure Hunt

 Hide a prize in the camp area. Then make a map showing where everything is. Make as many details as you can. Then put an "X" on the map where the hidden treasure is. Give the map to a friend and see if they can find the prize using your map.

Walking Stick with Bear Bells

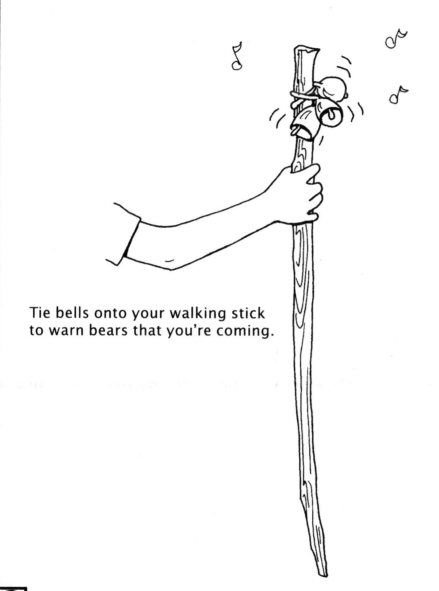

Tie bells onto your walking stick
to warn bears that you're coming.

MATERIALS

Straight branch or stick
4 metal bells,
about 1½ by 2 inches
Sturdy string or twine

Select a good walking stick; one that reaches to your shoulders should be about right. Peel off the bark if you want, and decorate it by carving or coloring it with markers.

When you choose your bells, test them to be sure they have a loud ring.

Lace the string through all the bells and tie a knot. Tie the string around the end of the stick.

While you are hiking with this walking stick, the bells will ring and alert any bears in the area that you are coming their way. You don't want to surprise bears—they may be frightened and feel threatened. Sing, whistle, talk loudly, and tie some bells to your walking stick so that they hear you coming.

Rattle Can

MATERIALS

Small tin can
String
Pebbles
Hammer and large nail
Duct tape

Stay Safe *Large animals can be dangerous! Don't go near them. Watch from a distance. A mother and baby are darling to see but remember that the mother will try to protect her young. Never walk between a mother and her baby.*

Good Idea *Take along a plastic bag when you hike. Collect trash and litter as you go along.*

Put in enough pebbles to make a lot of noise. Tape the top closed.

Make a handle out of string.

Have the camp cook save you a can. Wash it out with soap and warm water to get rid of the food odors. Make two holes in the can near the top with the hammer and nail. Make them directly across from each other, just below the rim.

Thread the string through the holes, and pull the ends of the string up so that they're even with each other. Knot the string near the top of the can, and then knot the ends of the string together.

Put enough pebbles in the can to make noise when you shake it. Tape the top opening of the can completely closed with duct tape. It will take several layers of tape over the hole to make it strong and secure.

Put your hand inside the loop of string and swing the can rattle as you hike along. This makes enough noise to warn animals before you frighten them on the trail.

Gather Some Potpourri

Stay Safe   *If you are hiking, collecting plants or picking berries, be sure the area hasn't been sprayed with poison chemicals. Logging companies spray areas to kill broad-leafed plants and shrubs. Roadways are often sprayed, too. If plants are sickly looking with yellow or brown leaves, or are dying, they may have been sprayed. The chemicals can make you sick, so find a different spot to enjoy.*

MATERIALS
Paper sack

A hike is the perfect time to gather natural materials to make potpourri when you get back home. Take along a paper sack and look for fragrant flower blossoms, tiny pinecones, dried mosses and lichens, beechnuts, wild roses, holly berries, sprigs of pine and spruce, seed heads from weeds, and pine needles. Just be careful not to take all the flowers or seed pods from one area. Select a few of each flower or weed; make sure to leave many untouched so that they can reseed new plants next year.

When you get home, mix in some cinnamon sticks, spices, and dried orange peel. Add a few drops of potpourri oil from a craft store to make it smell even more fragrant.

Store your potpourri in a glass jar or wrap some up in a piece of nylon net tied with a ribbon. Give some to a special friend.

Wild Berries

Berry Bucket

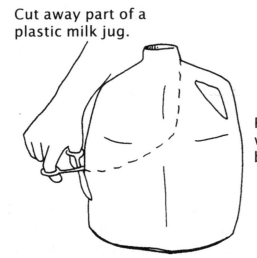

Cut away part of a plastic milk jug.

Fill your bucket with delicious berries.

Along your hike you may be able to find some wild berries to pick. Be sure an adult with you knows that the berries are safe. If they're not sure—don't pick them. Ask the campground manager or a forest ranger to identify berries for you. Poison berries look very tasty—but are very dangerous! Leave them for the birds and bears—they can eat them without getting sick.

If you are around wild berries, you may run into bears because they love berries, too. Be sure to make lots of noise along the trail or in the berry patch. Sing, whistle, or talk loudly or carry bells so a wild animal hears you first, and can run off without putting you in danger. If you are going to be in an area where bears are common, get a bear safety brochure from the National Park Service visitor's center.

MATERIALS

Plastic milk jug
Scissors
Belt

✸ Make a simple bucket to take along when you're berry picking. Cut a plastic jug as shown in the drawing. Hold it by the handle in one hand while you pick with the other. You can also thread your belt through the handle and use both hands for picking.

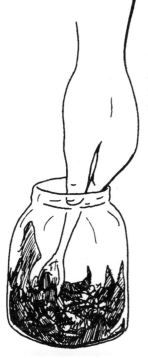

Mash berries with a spoon. Add water and stir. Spoon out the berry pulp.

Dip in your writing stick and write away.

Dear Jo...

MATERIALS

Fresh berries
Water
Pointed stick
Container, such as a baby food jar
Spoon

 Put the berries in the container and crush them with the spoon. Add some water and stir. Spoon out the berry pulp and use the tinted water that's left to write with. Dip a pointed stick into the berry ink and write a note to someone on paper. If you want to make the ink darker, mash in more berries.

You can also snip the end from a feather to make a quill pen.

Berry Ink and Stick Pen

Make berry ink just like Native Americans did long ago. Use a pointed stick to write with. Be sure you are using safe berries; poison berries can make you sick, *even if you only touch them.*

How Old Was That Tree?

Find a tree stump and count its rings. Each ring is one year in the life of that tree. Many trees are as old as 500 to 1,000 years old!

Look at each ring—is it thin or thick? When a ring is thin, the tree didn't grow much that year. This could be due to lack of rain or an early winter. If the ring is thick, the tree probably received a lot of water; there were good growing conditions that year. Look for dark rings. If you find a ring that is darker than the others, the tree probably survived a forest fire.

Count back to the year you were born. Can you find it? See if you can find a tree with 100 rings. Isn't it amazing how long it takes a tree to grow only a few inches around? Look for the years your mother and father were born, too.

There are many stories that this stump can tell. How many can you find?

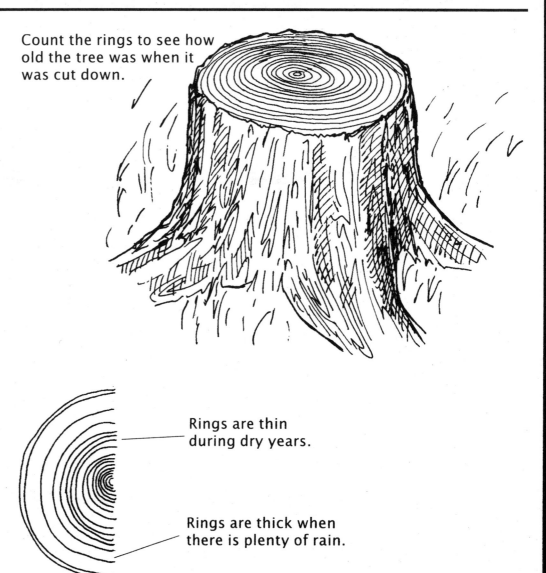

Count the rings to see how old the tree was when it was cut down.

Rings are thin during dry years.

Rings are thick when there is plenty of rain.

TIME TO EAT!

There's just something special about fresh air, sunshine, and the outdoors—when you're camping, you're *always* hungry! Without a refrigerator, sink, oven, or microwave, just fixing a snack may seem difficult. If you plan ahead and make a list of all the supplies you'll need for the meals you want to make, you should have plenty of tasty fun to look forward to. Read through these recipes before you leave home and write down the foods you'll need to take and the cooking or preparation equipment needed. Better yet, make a few of these snacks to munch on at home, just for practice. You may decide to fix them often, camping or not!

Shoebox Solar Oven

If you are camping during hot weather, you can make a sun oven to cook marshmallows, hot dogs, even s'mores! The best time to cook is midday, when the sun's rays are directly overhead and the hottest. This sun oven won't work on cloudy days.

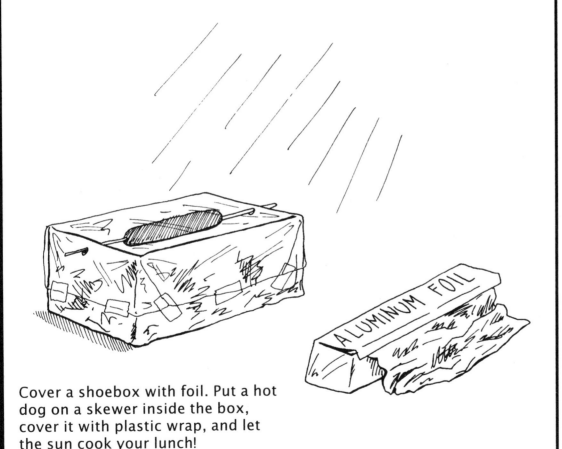

Cover a shoebox with foil. Put a hot dog on a skewer inside the box, cover it with plastic wrap, and let the sun cook your lunch!

MATERIALS

Shoebox
Aluminum foil
Wooden skewer
Plastic wrap
Tape
Marshmallows or hot dogs

Cover the inside and outside of the shoebox with aluminum foil, making sure that the shiny side of the foil shows. Tape it in place securely. Poke the wooden skewer into the marshmallows or hot dog, and push the skewer into each end of the box as shown in the illustration. Wrap plastic wrap tightly over the top of the box and tape in place. Put the sun oven in a sunny spot, and wait in the shade while the sun cooks your lunch.

You will want to turn the stick a little to be sure your food cooks on all sides. It will take a bit longer than in an electric oven, but you will be using only the sun's rays for energy.

S'mores

S'mores can be made by melting marshmallows on sticks over a campfire, then sandwiching them between graham crackers, with a bit of chocolate bar tucked inside. Here is a way to make s'mores anytime, or anywhere:

MATERIALS

1 chocolate candy bar
2 large graham crackers
2 large marshmallows
Aluminum foil

 Place a piece of the chocolate bar on top of one cracker. Place the marshmallows on top of the chocolate, and stack the other cracker on top. Wrap the whole thing up in foil (shiny side out) and put it in the solar oven, until the chocolate melts.

If you aren't using a solar oven, put the foil-wrapped s'mores in the sun for several minutes, until the chocolate melts.

You can even make s'mores on a rainy day at home! Put the foil-wrapped treats on a cookie sheet in a 250-degree oven and they will be ready in about 20 minutes.

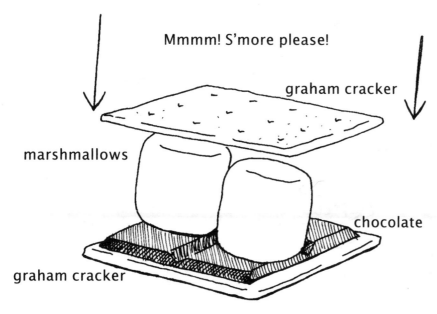

Mmmm! S'more please!

graham cracker

marshmallows

chocolate

graham cracker

Wrap it up in foil and let the sun melt it.

Cheesy Rice

MATERIALS

Cheese spread

1 cup cooked instant rice,
for each person

Spoon

Bowl

This is an easy dinner you can fix right away.

 Ask the camp cook to prepare a batch of instant rice for you, and while it's still hot, spoon on some cheese spread. Stir the cheese spread into the hot rice until it's melted. Add more to suit your taste. That's it. It's ready to eat!

It's an easy, cheesy treat.

Cheezy Spread

Mountain Man Sandwich Spread

MATERIALS

½ cup peanut butter
2 tablespoons honey
2 tablespoons bacon bits
1 tablespoon wheat germ
Small bowl
Spoon
Plastic container with lid

 Mix everything together and stir to blend. Add more honey if it's too stiff. Pack it into a covered container, or spread it on bread right away. This tastes really great when you top it with berry jam.

Wilderness Punch

MATERIALS

3 cups cold water
1 cup dry powdered milk
4 tablespoons orange drink mix
(like Tang)
Plastic container with lid

 Shake everything up in a covered plastic container. Add ice cubes if you have them.
   You can freeze the 3 cups of water in a plastic jug at home, then add the other stuff at camp as the ice melts. This will make it really cold.

Shake up a cold, refreshing beverage.

Cookies & Cream

MATERIALS

1 package instant pudding

⅓ cup dry powdered milk
and 1 cup cold water,
or 1 cup fresh milk

3 or 4 cookies

Plastic container with lid

Mix the instant pudding, water, and powdered milk in a plastic container with a lid. Shake it up to mix it. Crumble the cookies into the pudding and let it sit a few minutes to get thick. That's all!

Vanilla, banana, and tapioca pudding taste great with chocolate cookies. For vanilla cookies, try chocolate or butterscotch pudding. Experiment and come up with your own favorite combination.

Tutti Frutti

MATERIALS

1 package instant
pistachio pudding

½ cup dry powdered milk
and 1½ cups cold water,
or 1½ cups fresh milk

½ cup canned applesauce or
sliced banana

Handful of raisins and nuts, or
trail mix (see page 40)

Plastic container with lid
Spoon

Put the pudding, water, and powdered milk in a container with a lid. Shake until it's mixed. Stir in the apple-sauce, raisins and nuts. Let it sit a few minutes while it thickens.

Of course you can use regular milk instead of the dry powder and water.

Camp Cheesecake

This recipe makes about six servings.

Nature Note *Keep your food for yourself. It is tempting to feed the animals, but remember that their health depends on their own food. If an animal is fed by people it will lose its fear of people and could be easily killed by a hunter or a car.*

MATERIALS

1 package instant no-bake cheesecake mix

½ cup instant milk powder and 1¼ cup water, or 1½ cups fresh milk

⅓ cup squeezable margarine

2 bowls

2 forks

Pour the cheesecake filling into a camp bowl. Gradually add the milk to the filling, half a cup at a time. Stir with a fork to keep it from getting lumpy.

Mix the crumb mixture and the margarine in another bowl with a fork. Sprinkle the crumb mixture on top of the filling. Let it set for about 20 minutes in a shady spot.

This cheesecake won't be as stiff as cheesecake at home, but it will make a special dessert after dinner.

LIGHTS OUT!

When the sun starts to go down, camping *really* gets exciting! As the stars come out in the velvety night sky, you'll notice sights and sounds that can only be found in the outdoors at night. You'll notice so much more when you're away from the streetlights and the sounds of traffic. Nocturnal (night) animals come out looking for food and water, and calling on one another. While campers may find themselves getting sleepy and ready to turn in, the outdoors is just coming alive for deer, bats, raccoons, owls, and other animals that sleep during the day. Listen for their soft noises or the sharp howl of coyotes calling to one another.

With a warm quilt wrapped around you, and your friends and family around, the nighttime can be a time for telling tales, singing songs, or wondering at the stars in the sky.

Star Search

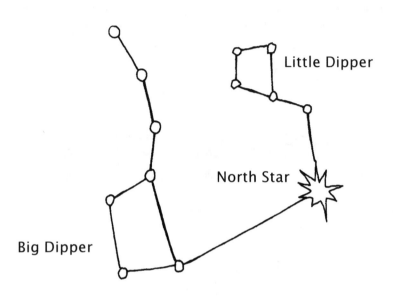

Little Dipper

North Star

Big Dipper

It's amazing what's up in the night sky, once you get away from the city lights!

Look up into the velvety darkness—at the glittering stars, and see if you can spot shapes made by the stars, called *constellations*.

The *Milky Way* is an almost solid, glittering band of white.

Can you find the *Big Dipper?* It's also called Ursa Major. The two outer stars of the Big Dipper point to the *Little Dipper,* which is harder to spot.

The *North Star,* also called Polaris, is at the tail end of the Little Dipper. With Polaris in front of you, you are facing north.

Shooting stars, or *falling stars,* are meteors. They give off light as they burn up when entering the earth's atmosphere. Meteor showers are the brightest after midnight. Some of the best times to watch for meteor showers are:

Delta Aquarids, July 28
Perseids, August 11
Orionids, October 19

The *Northern Lights,* also called Aurora Borealis, are spectacular during late-summer nights. They are yellow, pink, green, white and red, and look like nature's fireworks! Caused when the sun's rays hit the vacuum in the air above the earth, they sparkle and arc across the night sky. If you live in the northern U.S., Canada or Alaska, they show up very well, especially during years when sunspots have been common.

Nature Note The old-fashioned campfire can be exciting, but burning one uses wood from the campsite that could be left to decay or provide homes to small animals and insects. Outdoor burning also dirties the air and can be dangerous for you and the forest. Use a cookstove for meals. At night, use a fluorescent lantern, which everyone can gather around in the dark for story-telling, singing, or listening to coyotes.

Tall Tales in the Round

It's fun to tell stories—people enjoyed it for centuries before TV or radio—and camping makes it even more exciting. Sit in a circle and let one person begin the tale. They only make up a few sentences, then the person next to them adds to it. Everyone adds as the story goes around the circle.

Try to think of silly, exciting, scary or surprising things to add to keep it interesting. You'll be glad you didn't bring the TV!

Stay Safe *Check for ticks before you go to bed. If one is on you brush it off. If it has embedded in your skin, don't pull it or it's head may break off and remain in your skin. Use a cotton ball soaked in rubbing alcohol to suffocate it and make it lose its grip. After removing the tick, clean the bite area with antiseptic.*

Nature Note *Porcupines love salty, sweaty shoes, so take your shoes into the tent with you at night, or they may chew on them.*

Mysterious Moth Mixture

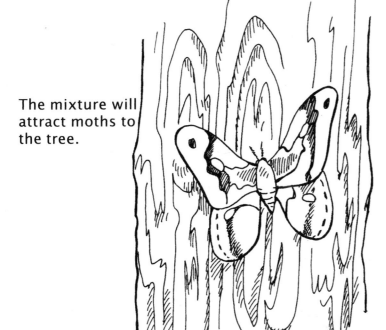

The mixture will attract moths to the tree.

MATERIALS

1 or 2 very ripe bananas, peaches or 1 cup of berries

1 cup fruit juice

4 tablespoons of sugar

Bowl

Fork

Flashlight

Paintbrush

Moths are very interesting, but you rarely get to see them because they are most active at night. Their colors make them hard to find in the daytime so their predators won't eat them while they rest. You can make some special food "paint" that moths will come to during the night, so you can get a close-up look at these beautiful creatures.

Mash the fruit in the bowl with a fork. Add the sugar to the fruit and mix. Gradually add the juice to the fruit mix stirring well with each addition of juice.

Paint the mixture onto at least three trees well away from your tent. Ask the landowner or campground attendant for permission to paint the trees first and use this paint only where there are no bears because the food paint will also attract bears.

Make a map of the area to help you remember which trees are painted with the mixture.

When it is night and fully dark go out with a flashlight and check the trees to see what moths and insects were attracted.

SAY GOODBYE

When it's time to leave, there are lots of chores to do. Wait till the morning dew dries on the tent before packing it up so it won't mold at home. Brush dirt and pine needles off the tent, tarps, and sleeping bags before folding them up, too. If you had a campfire, make sure it's completely out. Douse it with water and cover it with sand before you go.

Clean up the campsite, taking everything you brought with you. Try to leave it cleaner than when you arrived.

Take one last look around the area, to be sure nothing is forgotten and left behind, and to take a "mental snapshot" of your lovely campsite.

> **Good Idea**   *Remember to "protect and respect" the outdoors.*

Take Home a Tree

MATERIALS

Tree seeds

Rotting leaves, twigs, and other things from the forest ground

Plastic container with lid

 Wouldn't it be nice to have a lovely tree growing in your yard at home, to remind you of the forest? But should you dig up a little tree to take home? Young tree seedlings don't often survive if dug up and replanted, and where would our next forest come from if everyone dug up a tree and carried it off? Instead of digging up a tree, search for a seed to take home and plant.

Trees scatter thousands of seeds each year. Some are eaten by tiny animals, some fall in the wrong place and dry up or freeze, and some grow into trees. Taking one or two seeds home won't harm the forest, and you can enjoy a tree in your yard for years to come.

Seeds from pine, maple, linden, birch, and oak won't sprout if you plant them as soon as you get home. They need a cold winter to sprout, so use the refrigerator to chill them.

While you are at camp, fill a plastic container with rotting leaves, twigs, and debris from the forest ground. Add your seeds and close the container tightly. Before you put this container in the refrigerator, sprinkle a bit of water on the leaves.

Leave it in the refrigerator for about 3 months. Then you can fill a pot with rich soil and plant the seeds.

Something to Remember

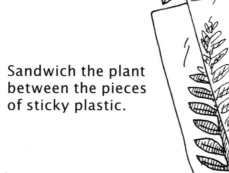

Sandwich the plant between the pieces of sticky plastic.

Punch holes and knot loops of yarn or ribbon to the ends.

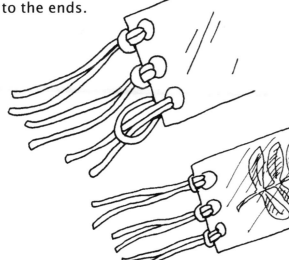

Use your bookmark to remind you of the fun you had camping—or give it to someone special.

MATERIALS

Clear plastic adhesive paper
(like Contac)

If you take along some clear plastic peel-and-stick paper you can bring home a special flower or delicate fern frond to use as a bookmark. Every time you use it you'll remember the fun you had in the great outdoors.

Cut two pieces of the plastic about 2 by 4 inches, leaving the paper backing on until you find the perfect bloom. Then peel the paper backing away from the sticky plastic and center the flower between the two layers of plastic. Press out the bubbles and wrinkles.

When you get home, trim the edges neatly with scissors. Punch a couple of holes in the end and knot on lengths of delicate ribbon or yarn.

RESOURCES

Addresses & Phone Numbers

National Park Service
Dept. of Interior Building
Washington, DC 20240

Go Camping America
1-800-47-SUNNY
(Call for a free camping
   vacation planner.)

Kampgrounds of America (KOA)
P.O. Box 30558
Billings, MT 59114-0558
(Send $3.00 for a directory
   listing their campgrounds.)

State travel bureaus have information on campsites and state parks. Write or call the state you plan to camp in for information.

U.S. Fish and Wildlife Service

Pacific Region
911 NE 11th Avenue
Portland, OR 97323-4181
(CA, HI, ID, NV, WA)

Southwest Region
P.O. Box 1306
Albuquerque, NM 87103
(AZ, NM, OK, TX)

North-Central Region
Federal Building
Fort Snelling
Twin Cities, MN 55111
(IL, IN, IA, MI, MN, MO, OH, WI)

Southeast Region
75 Spring Street S.W., Room 1200
Atlanta, GA 30303
(AL, AR, FL, GA, KY, MS, NC, SC,
  TN, PR, VI)

Northeast Region
1 Gateway Center, Suite 700
Newton Corner, MA 02158
(CT, DC, ME, MD, MA, NH, NJ,
  NY, PA, RI, VT, VA, WV)

Rocky Mountain Region
P.O. Box 25486 DFC
Denver, CO 80225
(CO, KS, MT, ND, NE, SD, UT, WY)

Alaska Region
1011 E. Tudor Road
Anchorage, AK 99503

Bureau of Land Management

Alaska State Office
222 W. Seventh Avenue, #13
Anchorage, AK 99513-7599

Arizona State Office
3707 N. Seventh Street
Phoenix, AZ 85011

California State Office
2800 Cottage Way, Room E-2845
Sacramento, CA 95825

Colorado State Office
2850 Youngfield Road
Lakewood, CO 80215

Eastern State Office
350 S. Pickett Street
Alexandria, VA 22304

Idaho State Office
3380 Americana Terrace
Boise, ID 83706

Montana State Office
0P.O. Box 36800
Billings, MT 59107

Nevada State Office
P.O. Box 12000
Reno, NV 89520-0006

New Mexico State Office
P.O. Box 1449
Santa Fe, NM 87504

Oregon State Office
P.O. Box 2965
Portland, OR 97208

Utah State Office
P.O. Box 45155
Salt Lake City, UT 84145-0155

Wyoming State Office
P.O. Box 1828
Cheyenne, WY 82003

National Park Services

Alaska Regional
2525 Gambell Street, Room 107
Anchorage, AK 99503-2892

Harpers Ferry Center
Harpers Ferry, WV 25425

Mid-Atlantic Regional
143 S. Third Street
Philadelphia, PA 19106

Midwest Regional
1709 Jackson Street
Omaha, NE 68102

National Capitol Region
1100 Ohio Drive S.W.
Washington, D.C. 20242

North-Atlantic Regional
15 State Street, Eighth Floor
Boston, MA 02109-3572

Pacific Northwest Regional
83 S. King Street, Suite 212
Seattle, WA 98104

Rocky Mountain Regional
P.O. Box 25287
Denver, CO 80225

Southwest Regional
P.O. Box 728
Santa Fe, NM 87504-0728

Books

Audubon Society Field Guides are available at bookstores and cover the following areas:

Birds
Butterflies
Fishes, Whales, and Dolphins
Fossils
Mammals
Rocks and Minerals
Seashells
Seashore Creatures
Trees
Wildflowers

Write for information from:

National Audubon Society
950 Third Avenue
New York, NY 10022

The *Boy Scout Handbook* and other guides can be purchased from your local Boy Scouts of America Council, listed in the telephone directory white pages. Or write to the national office:

Boy Scouts of America
13225 Walnut Hill Lane
Irving, TX 75038-3096

The U.S. Forest Service has detailed posters of birds, fish, trees, and plants. Look in the telephone directory under "Government Offices, U.S." for a local office. It's part of the Department of Agriculture. If there is no office in your area, you can write to the national office for information:

U.S. Forest Service
USDA
Washington, D.C. 20250

Other field guides include *Peterson's Guide to Birds* and *Peterson's Guide to Wildflowers* from Houghton Mifflin Company.

Another useful book is *North American Wildlife* from Readers' Digest Books. All are available in bookstores.

Write to the address below for a list of publications; many are useful to campers.

Superintendent of Documents
U.S. Government Printing Office
Washington, D.C. 20402

More Books by Laurie Carlson from Chicago Review Press

Green Thumbs
A Kid's Activity Guide to Indoor and Outdoor Gardening

With a few seeds, some water and soil, and this book, kids will be creating gardens of their own in no time. They will also create compost, make watering cans, mix up bug sprays, lay slug traps, grow crazy cucumbers, and much more.

ages 3–9
ISBN 1-55652-238-X
144 pages, paper, $12.95

Huzzah Means Hooray
Activities from the Days of Damsels, Jesters, and Blackbirds in a Pie

Kids can re-create a long-ago world of kings, castles, jousts, jesters, magic fairies, and Robin Hood—all they need are their imaginations and materials they can find at home.

ages 3–9
ISBN 1-55652-227-4
184 pages, paper, $12.95

More Than Moccasins
A Kid's Activity Guide to Traditional North American Indian Life

Kids will discover traditions and skills handed down from the people who first settled this continent, including how to plant a garden, make useful pottery, and communicate through Navajo code talkers.

"As an educator who works with Indian children I highly recommend [More Than Moccasins] for all kids and teachers…I learned things about our Indian world I did not know."

—Bonnie Jo Hunt
Wicahpi Win (Star Woman)
Standing Rock Lakota

ages 3–9
ISBN 1-55652-213-4
200 pages, paper, $12.95